Mary:
When God Shares His Glory

CHRIST JOHN OTTO

MARY
When God Shares His Glory

Book 2 in the
THRONE IN THE EARTH SERIES
on the Arts, the Ark and the Word made Flesh.

Mary: When God Shares His Glory

Book Two in the Throne in the Earth Series on the Arts, the Ark, and the Word Made Flesh

Copyright © 2016 by Christ John Otto. Edited by Nancy Mari. All rights reserved. Published by Belonging House Creative

Visit www.belonginghouse.org.

Scripture quotations, unless otherwise noted, are from The Revised Standard Version of the Bible: Catholic Edition, copyright © 1965, 1966 the Division of Christian Education of the National Council of the Churches of Christ in the United States of America. Used by permission. All rights reserved.

Scripture quotations marked (NLT) are taken from the Holy Bible, New Living Translation, copyright ©1996, 2004, 2007, 2013 by Tyndale House Foundation. Used by permission of Tyndale House Publishers, Inc., Carol Stream, Illinois 60188. All rights reserved.

Scripture quotations marked (NRSVA) are taken from the New Revised Standard Version Bible: Anglicized Edition, copyright © 1989, 1995 the Division of Christian Education of the National Council of the Churches of Christ in the United States of America. Used by permission. All rights reserved.

*To
Father Al
Father Dean
Father Mary Louis
and
Father Timothy.
From you I received grace. Thanks.*

O Lord, I am your servant;
I am your servant and the child of your handmaid;
you have freed me from my bonds. —Psalm 116:16

TABLE OF CONTENTS

	Introduction: A Way Forward	ix
ONE	Show Me Your Glory	1
TWO	Lost Glory	5
THREE	Glory	9
FOUR	Theme and Variations	21
FIVE	God-Bearer	29
SIX	Grace	35
SEVEN	Ark	45
EIGHT	Blessed	55
NINE	Woman	63
TEN	Bride	73
ELEVEN	Crowned	83
TWELVE	Offspring	95
	Postlude	107
	Acknowledgments	109
	Works Cited	111

MARY

INTRODUCTION: A WAY FORWARD

For the past few months I have been living in Scotland and two stories have dominated the news. The United Kingdom voted to leave the European Union. In the United States there is a protracted unsettling Presidential election. These nations are experiencing a transition, and something is happening. In many ways we are experiencing the end of the government of man. Hopefully, we are seeing the emergence of the Government of God in the earth.

Five hundred years ago, something similar began to happen in Western Civilization. I call it the "500 Year Cycle."

Every 500 years Western Civilization goes through a shift. These shifts are profound and take roughly a century to accomplish. If we look back in time, these rough demarcations can easily be identified. When we review history, we see that the Hellenistic era, and the flowering of Greek culture and thought began around 500 BC. This was right around the time that Darius released the Jews from captivity in Babylon and they returned to their homeland. Five hundred years later the Roman Empire emerged, Jesus Christ was born and Jewish and Greek cultures together birthed Christianity. Five hundred years later the Western Roman empire collapsed and Europe entered a Dark Age. Out of that transition emerged the monastic movements that transformed Europe. Five hundred years later the Franks invaded Britain, the Vikings were Christianized, and the Great Schism between the Eastern and Western Church happened. And five hundred years later The Renaissance, the Protestant Reformation, and Western Imperialism began.

MARY

Yes, I just recapped 2000 years in a paragraph.

Here we are, Five hundred years later, and our world is going through a cataclysm. It's hard to get perspective about events that are so close, but in the last one hundred years the two largest wars in human history occurred, two plagues—cancer and HIV/AIDS—have ravaged millions of people, the Roman Catholic Church called the second Vatican Council and embraced nearly all the reforms demanded by Martin Luther, and we have experienced a technological revolution that is beginning to eclipse even the imaginations of science fiction. And in some ways it looks like the West is heading into another dark age. All this change is causing an identity crisis.

I devoted a lot of space in my book *An Army Arising* to the history of Christianity and this cycle, and how it determined the role of the artist.

Over the past decade the role of art and artists in this new world has become more and more pronounced. As I often hear, "design is the message." In this new 500 year cycle the international language is visual and multi-sensory. As I wrote in my last book, creative people are priests to a visual-digital culture.

When I am invited to speak in a new location, I begin with this introduction:

> We live in an increasingly multimedia world. The Church has sidelined the arts, but in doing so she has been sidelined by the culture. Imagine a world where artists and creative people are truly disciples of Jesus Christ. In that world the magazine covers would be different. TV shows would be different. Drama would be different. Radio programming would be

different. Song lyrics would be different. Clothing would be different and even the paint color and furniture in this room would be different because artists touch every area of life. In today's world there is no such thing as a starving artist, unless they take advice from an ill informed person and go out and try to find a "real job."

Artists and creative people, who I have labeled "the culture shapers," are now in the center.

The Right Question

In each of these 500 year transitions, the people who live in the West begin to ask questions. In the last cycle, the big question became "What must I do to be saved?" This question became the foundation of all the changes and doctrines of the Protestant Reformation. And most of the decisions made at that time were about defining and clarifying who is saved, how one becomes saved, and how one stays saved.

The church made some wonderful gains because of the Reformation. Both Protestants and Catholics eventually gained a deeper appreciation for the Bible. Basic standards of education and morality were set for church leadership. A global missions movement (both Catholic and Protestant) was birthed. Western Civilization was transformed.

Here we are at a crossroad. And today people are beginning to ask different questions. Those questions are:

Do I have value?
Where do I belong?

And as many church leaders are discovering, even when they make their Reformation answers more culturally relevant, or media savvy, they still are not providing the answers to these two questions.

People are leaving the church, but not out of a rejection of the gospel. They are leaving because they are hungry and they are looking for bread. Hungry people go where they hope to find food. Proverbs 27:7 tells us "Those who are full loathe honey, but to the hungry even bitter things are sweet." People are willing to try lifestyles and religions that bring death in the hope that they can meet this deep hunger.

Many of the church leaders I know are answering questions no one is asking. And I should add that this is killing a lot of leaders because they really want to answer the right questions. The vast majority of pastors and church leaders love people. They work very hard trying to provide bread for the world, and many of them are mystified that so few are interested.

Making Peace

Pablo Picasso once said the first act of creation is an act of destruction. Although I may not agree on how Picasso applied this statement, I do agree with the "nugget of truth" it contains. An artist or creative person always sees what's missing or broken in a situation and then begins the work of repair and restoration. Because of the innate ability to see what is wrong with something, creative people often tend to be unpopular—especially with those who are invested in keeping things the way they are—the status quo.

Creative people see what's broken or missing.

This is one of the reasons creative people are often described as being overly critical or having an "artistic temperament."

The Hebrew word we translate "peace" is the word *shalom*. A very basic definition of this word is "nothing broken, nothing missing." Peace is the presence of order, not an absence of conflict. Let me say that again:

INTRODUCTION: A WAY FORWARD

Peace is the presence of order not the absence of conflict.

If a creative person sees what's broken or missing, then they are called to create Shalom. Creative people are designed to repair and restore what is broken and missing in the world. Making shalom is the greatest creative act. Ultimately, all creative people are called to be peacemakers.

When we hear Jesus say in the Beatitudes "Blessed are the peacemakers," we have been trained to hear "blessed are the peace*keepers*." Making Shalom is a risky act that requires incredible creativity. When you make peace you are attempting to find a way forward where there has not been one before—because the path has been broken or missing. Often conflicts arise when relationships are broken or the truth is hidden or distorted.

Peacekeeping is not a creative act. Peacekeeping forces people to accept broken systems or situations. Peacekeeping forces everyone involved to give up something for the greater good. Peacekeeping requires you to make do with a broken system "because this is the way things are." Peacekeeping makes you a victim. At the heart of peacekeeping is compromise—each side has to give up something to keep bullets from flying. The systems peacekeepers create are marked by their unsatisfactory lukewarm cultures. Peacekeeping demands accepting things as they always have been. Peacekeeping never calls into question the status quo. Peacekeeping is a temporary fix. Sadly, eventually people get tired of surrendering their values and dreams and the guns get loaded and the bullets fly.

Peacemaking, on the other hand, begins with "this is what's broken or missing." Peacemaking requires an honest assessment. Then peacemakers, creative people, begin the difficult task of finding a new way forward. Being honest is unpopular. This is when those who have "never done it that way before" begin to attack the creative person. These good people represent the Status Quo. In the eyes of the Status Quo the enemy is not the problem. The enemy is the problem solver. The enemy is the person brave enough to assess a situation and suggest a solution. Shalom always requires us to make a change. We have to change our thinking, change our choices, and change the way we do things. As Seth Godin said in one of his recent daily blogs, "Change begins when you imagine a different kind of future." That's pretty close to what the Bible calls "repentance."

The Ability to See

One of the important lessons I learned as an applied artist was the ability to see. A good draftsman can look at an object and break it down into its component shapes and "see" what is really there. Drawing is not creating a bunch of lines. Drawing is laying down boundaries around shapes and shadows.

Repeatedly creative artists are called "prophetic" individuals. They tend to run ahead of the crowd and forge a way forward. I think it is interesting that the original word for prophet in Hebrew was "seer." **The prophet is the one who sees.**

A good artist immediately sees what's wrong. This is why many creative people are so grumpy—and why so many suffer from depression.

Without the freedom to acknowledge a problem and find a solution an artist will get stuck in the destruction phase, and that destruction will turn inward. First it becomes depression and then worse.

Being an artist has taught me another thing: **Many people can look at something all day long and not see what is really there.** The conventional crowd is often blind, and can be deceived. This is the

INTRODUCTION: A WAY FORWARD

realm of the illusionist, magician, and the modern politician. People look at things based on their preconceptions, and this weakness can be used and abused. This blindness is part of what drives peacekeeping. To a person without the ability to see it is much safer to live with the way things are.

All people have a God-given desire to make things better, but most believe that they are powerless to do so. In order to get along people try to keep peace and not make waves. Making peace requires the ability to see and the courage to make change.

When we make peace, find a way forward, and come up with a creative solution, we suddenly find that God has been doing a work of healing and transformation in our lives. Keeping peace with brokenness keeps us from growing and going forward. Making peace is scary, because we have to face the truth.

This book is about making peace with Mary and how God became flesh.

God became a man. This is one of the foundational beliefs of the Christian faith. It is also the one belief that sets Christianity apart from every other worldview and religion. If you are an artist, it is the most important of all the Christian doctrines. This idea, called the "Incarnation," is what makes your calling possible, and valid. God becoming flesh changes you from being an idol-maker to being an iconographer. God becoming flesh changes the artist from one who leads people into pagan darkness into one who leads people into an encounter with the Living God.

After Bezalel, Mary is the most important person in the Bible when it comes to the arts. She is the only person in all of creation who actually made the word flesh. In fact, it was her flesh that took on the Word. And because of this the barriers between flesh and spirit, time and eternity, God and humanity, all blurred.

Making Peace with Mary

In the first book of this series I looked at Bezalel and his mission to build a portable throne for God in the earth. This throne, the Ark of the Covenant, forms a gold thread through the Bible. Instead of following the Ark chronologically, we are going to jump into the New Testament and see how the Ark becomes linked with Mary, the mother of Jesus. We are going to look at what is broken and missing in our view of Mary. Bringing Shalom to artists and creative people is the main purpose for this book.

A study of Mary should help us get greater understanding of Jesus and our identity in him. In a unique way, Mary straddles both realities. Mary did touch heaven and earth.

This is a series about the Word becoming flesh. Every creative person makes the unseen tangible. Mary, more than any other person in human history, demonstrated this reality. To ignore this ripple in the space-time continuum is to miss all that God has to say about our physical reality, all the Bible has to say about women, motherhood and family, and the astounding way God is redeeming a renegade creation.

Hold on tight, this book might re-arrange your reality. Hopefully, if you are an artist, you will then begin rearranging reality for others.

Christ John Otto,
Edinburgh, Scotland
2016

ONE

SHOW ME YOUR GLORY

Every story has a beginning.

This story begins on a mountain top, and in a funny way, is directly related to the misuse of the arts.

Moses spent 40 days on the mountain with God. In those forty days God gave Moses the plans for an interactive art installation. It would be a worship center that was essentially an embassy of heaven on earth. And in the center of this embassy was a throne room where a portable throne for God would reside on the earth. And at the end of the 40 days God commissioned an artist, Bezalel, to create everything according to the plan.

Meanwhile, Aaron was creating a golden calf for the people to worship.

In the aftermath of the story of the golden calf, Moses pleads with God on behalf of the people. In his intercession Moses makes one personal request: "Show me your glory."

The only cure for the false is the true. Moses had seen the false worship of Israel, and after encountering it, he needed a refresher. He needed to be brought back into the Presence of God.

Moses is instructed to go up on the mountain, and God promises that he will be protected from the sheer intensity of the glory. God was going to display something never before seen by a human being.

MARY

The power that was going to be displayed was so great that even animals were not permitted to graze near the mountain.

And then God came and passed by Moses in all his glory.

And in the glory God speaks to us about himself. We discover the identity of God.

> "The Lord, the Lord,
>   a God merciful and gracious,
>   slow to anger,
>   and abounding in steadfast love and faithfulness,
>   keeping steadfast love for the thousandth generation,
>   forgiving iniquity and transgression, and sin,
>   yet by no means clearing the guilty,
>   but visiting the iniquity of the parents upon the children,
>   and the children's children to the third and fourth generation."[1]

Whenever we encounter the glory, we encounter the identity of God. And we find out something really surprising about God's nature.

God works through families. One righteous person can influence a thousand generations. Fathers, mothers, and children become the conduits of God's mercy and grace. This story is about people, and about how one person's "yes" to God can impact a thousand generations.

The person was Mary. This book is about how Mary encountered the glory of God, and in the encounter said yes to a scary proposition. Her story is ultimately about how God makes the word flesh. It's about how God creates. If you are a creative person, then there is a lot you need to learn from Mary.

---

1 Exodus 34:6-7.

SHOW ME YOUR GLORY

Whenever you encounter the glory of God you encounter a part of God's identity. And in the encounter you begin to experience a transformation in your own identity. The glory and identity go together.

The glory is essential to understanding a core piece of the New Covenant. Jesus has shared his glory with you. And in that transaction "a new Creation" emerges. You are a new creation that contains the glory. Your inner life, touched by the glory, determines your creative output.

The New Testament is full of verses that paint a picture of what a life in the glory looks like. Jesus prayed for us to have this experience, and Paul lays a doctrinal foundation for a life in the glory. But there is only one person in Scripture who lived her life before us as an example.

Mary is the model of a life that has been touched by the glory. If we look at her life we suddenly see how repeated encounters with the glory change a person.

Moses came down from the mountain after his glory moment and Exodus tells us that his face shone with the glory he encountered. And out of his encounter the most creative act of his life emerged—the building of the Tabernacle. God shared his glory with Moses and Moses shared that glory with Bezalel. And Bezalel created the Ark.

As I said, God works through families and generations and tribes. Mary was part of the tribe of Bezalel. And she becomes a living embodiment of the Ark Bezalel built. This is her story, the story of becoming in God, becoming a throne for God in the earth, and becoming who you truly are as you encounter the glory.

MARY

TWO

LOST GLORY

Although this story began with Moses, there is a long "back story" to our story.

It begins with the first story in the Bible. There was the man, created from the dust of the earth. He was given charge over an incredible garden, and he was given the job of naming every plant and animal in the garden. One fascinating thing about the sciences is their need to name every newly discovered animal and plant. We are still discovering and naming. This was that first commandment given to Adam.

God observed the man, and soon it was clear that he was lonely. He needed another person that he could relate to.

So God put the man into a deep sleep. God opened the man's side, and removed a rib. Out of this bone he made a woman. The rabbis talk a lot about how significant this was. She was not from his head—to have power over him. She was not from his feet, to be subjected under him. She was from his side so that she could walk beside him and be his help mate. They were to walk together. And something about this relationship was designed to reflect God's glory.

MARY

And when the man awoke, he met the woman of his dreams.

> Then the man said, "This at last is bone of my bones and flesh of my flesh; she shall be called Woman, because she was taken out of Man."[2]

So this first female of the human race was first known as Woman before she received her name. And the man and the woman received their first commandment as a couple: "Be fruitful and multiply, and fill the earth and subdue it."

There is a tendency to assume that the man and the woman were only told to procreate, and certainly this is part of this command. They were told to have children. But there is another dimension to this command. They were to be fruitful. They were to create. They were to be like their Creator, and become little creators, ones who shared a measure of the glory of the one who made them.

A core part of being human is to create.

And then something happens. Out on a walk, the woman encounters a wily creature, the Serpent. And she begins to have a conversation with him. We don't know if the Serpent spoke to the woman numerous times. But we do know that the woman entered into the conversation, and let the Serpent distort God's command to eat of all the trees of the forest except one. The Serpent lied to the woman, and the woman ate of the tree that should not be eaten. And some of the light in her went out, and some of the glory that she carried dimmed. And then the woman did something even more treacherous. She went to the man and interceded on behalf of the Serpent, and she persuaded her husband to believe the same lie she had believed.

---

2   Genesis 2:23.

LOST GLORY

And then the eyes of both were opened, and they went from glory to grey. They experienced shame, remorse, and the need to cover up. And then they ran from God.

There have been millions of books, sermons, and retellings of this story. This story is the conflict established for the drama that unfolds over the rest of the Bible. This story establishes the plot of the story of redemption, and the story we are going to talk about in this book.

Because the woman made a choice she lost the glory endowed by her creator. And God, recognizing that the woman interacted with the Serpent, makes a chilling statement to the Tempter.

> I will put enmity between you and the woman, between your offspring and hers; he will strike your head and you will strike his heel.[3]

In this cryptic statement God promises that he would use a woman, and her child would undo this moment of lost glory. Genesis 3:15 is the first "Messianic" promise in the Bible.

After the Fall the man finally names his woman. He gives her the name Eve, because she will be the mother of all the living. She is to be the bringer of life.

But, because of the lost glory, something different happens. Eve's first child is a murderer. Rather than bringing life, Eve gives birth to the shedding of innocent blood. As we will see over and over, because of sin, we have a "discreative" world rather than a creative world. We make things that are distorted, corrupted, or off base,

---

3   Genesis 3:15.

MARY

rather than creative. These things are not outright destruction, but they leave destruction in their wake. It is often the law of unintended consequences that gets us into trouble. This is what happens when the glory disappears.

Embedded in the promise of Genesis 3:15 is the role a woman was going to play in the undoing of Eve's mistake. We are going to observe how over time the glory is going to be regained, but before we do, we need to talk a little about what the glory is and how that glory is going to be restored.

In the next two chapters, let's take a look at some key concepts in order to understand the story of Mary, her identity, and how it relates to the glory.

THREE

GLORY

Before we go too deep into the story of Mary, and how God transformed her identity into the one who made the Word flesh, we have to take some time to talk about glory. What is the glory?

The short answer is, the glory is an extension of the Person, Presence, and Power of God.

When we talk about the glory, and actually any of the ideas that encompass "theology" and "doctrine," where you begin is very important. If you begin in the wrong place, all your conclusions will be distorted.

Hebrew not Greco-Roman

One of the central concepts of the New Testament, well, the Bible as a whole really, is the glory of God. When you do an in depth study of the words the Bible uses to describe God's glory, you suddenly begin to understand a lot about the God the Bible reveals. This God is very different from the god of the Greek philosophers. The Greek philosophers described God in impersonal terms based on the attributes they believed a perfect being would have—this god is all-powerful, all-knowing, a force that could not be moved, but moved others. This is very different from the God described in the Bible. Paul noted that the god the philosophers described was an "Unknown God." The Bible talks about God from a position of knowing. This God has a name: YHWH "I AM."

MARY

This God with a name is described in personal terms—not in the terms of classical philosophy. The Bible does not begin with God is sovereign, God is omnipotent (all-powerful), omniscient (all-knowing), omnipresent (everywhere at once) or immutable (an unmoved mover). None of these terms appear in the Bible, at least in the original languages. These are all Greco-Roman ideas put on the Bible. Some of them do describe aspects of God, but they are impersonal terms and the God of the Bible is intensely personal. None of them adequately describes Him.

The same goes for glory. The Greco-Roman concept of glory is really closer to the word "fame." It is renown, celebrity, and accolades, all usually given based on performance. This kind of glory comes from victory in battle, winning a contest, or an election. And this kind of glory is given to someone by others. Glory in this sense is about something you do, rather than who you are. It is performance over substance.

Weird things happen when you begin with the Greco-Roman concept of "glory," marry it to the impersonal philosopher's god, and begin to apply it to human situations. You have a god who doesn't help you when you are suffering. You have a god who sets the clock running and then leaves to let it tend itself. You have a god who gets glory from people being sick, and who gets glory from sending people to hell. And when something bad happens, the question becomes "Why did God allow bad things to happen to good people?" The "Why?" question is really a condemnation of a god who is out of touch. This god is a causer of pain rather than a redeemer of pain. This god is a stoic, emotionless, distant authority figure who is an all-seeing eye but never reaches out and touches. This kind of god is not biblical at all, and completely misrepresents the Father of Jesus.

Glory in the Bible is about God revealing a part of who He is.

GLORY

Every time God's glory manifests, it is a moment of self-revelation. Remember the encounter Moses had with the glory on the mountain. God first begins describing himself to Moses. The Glory of God always tells us something about who He is. You cannot separate the glory of God from God's Person, Presence, or Power. And God does not get glory from outward things. God is the source of his own Glory. Any glory we give to Him was first given to us by Him. As one of my mentors in prayer, Dr. Margaret Therkelson described, it is a "love exchange." Remember, the New Covenant begins with "God is Love."

God's glory is always about his Person, Presence, and Power. And He is the source of his own glory.

Weight

The New Testament word for "glory" is *doxa*. It is pronounced DOKE-sa. Doxa was the word used in ancient Greek for opinion or belief. It still comes to us today in the word "orthodox" or "right belief." When the Hebrew Bible was first translated into Greek, the translators took this word and re-defined it. They used doxa to translate the Hebrew word *kabod*. (Pronounced ka-BODE.)

The kabod is the weighty presence of God. It is the thing that makes God impressive. And whenever you encounter the kabod, you are encountering a portion of God's identity. "Since God is invisible, it necessarily carries a reference to his self-manifestation."[4]

Let me say that again:

Whenever you encounter the glory, you are encountering a part of God's identity.

---

4   Theological Dictionary of the New Testament, 178.

If we follow the kabod throughout the Bible, we see a number of things linked to God's glory: lightning and thunder,[5] and the heavenly realms.[6] In Exodus God's glory is revealed as a cloud, a pillar, and the radiant substance that fills the tabernacle and dwells between the wings of the cherubim. Moses' face shines when he is exposed to it. The Glory is a thing, not an idea.

"In Ezekiel's visions the glory of God is personified. The glory rides on a throne, has a human shape, bears very strongly the characteristics of light, and both leaves the first temple and returns to the second."[7]

And finally, and this is important, God says that Israel has glory because God is in their midst. **God shares his glory with Israel.**[8] Something about God's identity is revealed through these chosen people. And if the glory is part of God's identity, then God is sharing a part of his personhood with Israel. God identifies with people.

The Glory in People

God always wanted to share his glory. Listen to this promise from the end of the book of Zephaniah:

> The LORD, your God, is in your midst, a warrior who gives victory; he will rejoice over you with gladness, he will renew you in his love; he will exult over you with loud singing as on a day of festival. "I will remove disaster from you, so that you will not bear reproach for it. Behold, at that time I will deal with all

---

5   Psalms 97, 29, Ezekiel 1.

6   Psalm 19:1.

7   TDNT, 179.

8   Zechariah 2:5-9.

GLORY

your oppressors. And I will save the lame and gather the outcast, and I will change their shame into praise and renown in all the earth.

At that time I will bring you home, at the time when I gather you together; yea, I will make you renowned and praised among all the peoples of the earth, when I restore your fortunes before your eyes," says the Lord.[9]

Whenever you see God's Person, Presence or Power, you are seeing manifestation of the glory. At the end of Zephaniah we get a New Covenant promise that when the Presence of God is in the midst of his people God is going to release a number of things. Because of the glory, God promises to rejoice over you. God promises to sing songs over you. God promises to protect you. God promises to bring healing, take away shame, and bring financial abundance. All of these things are the outworking of the Glory of God in your midst.

When we get into the New Testament, God's glory takes on a new dimension. In the New Testament we get references to human beings carrying the *kabod*, the *doxa*, the glory of God. Jesus takes the manifestation of God to a whole new level. It should be no surprise that his birth is greeted by angels declaring "Glory to God in the Highest."

Jesus is
- raised from the dead by the glory (Romans 6:4)
- taken up into glory (I Timothy 3:16)
- seated at the right hand of glory (Acts 7:55)
- the Lord of glory (I Corinthians 2:8)
- the hope of glory (Titus 2:13)

---

9 Zephaniah 3:17-20.

MARY

In the Gospel of John the manifestation of Jesus in the incarnation, at his crucifixion, and resurrection are all marked with references to glory, glorification, and the manifestation of glory.

In Jesus a human being becomes the carrier of glory.

And then the New Testament writers, but especially Paul, really mess with things. In Romans chapter 8 Paul gives us a window into the glory in the life of a believer:

> So then, brethren, we are debtors, not to the flesh, to live according to the flesh—for if you live according to the flesh you will die, but if by the Spirit you put to death the deeds of the body you will live. For all who are led by the Spirit of God are sons of God. For you did not receive the spirit of slavery to fall back into fear, but you have received the spirit of sonship. When we cry, "Abba! Father!" it is the Spirit himself bearing witness with our spirit that we are children of God, and if children, then heirs, heirs of God and fellow heirs with Christ, provided we suffer with him in order that we may also be glorified with him.
>
> I consider that the sufferings of this present time are not worth comparing with the glory that is to be revealed to us. For the creation waits with eager longing for the revealing of the sons of God; for the creation was subjected to futility, not of its own will but by the will of him who subjected it in hope; because the creation itself will be set free from its bondage to decay and obtain the glorious liberty of the children of God.[10]

---

10 Romans 8:12-21.

God plans to share his glory with you. God wants you to reflect his radiant holiness, and to bear his weighty Presence, Person, and Power. There is so much more.

Jesus actually says this clearly in the prayer recorded in John 17.

> The glory that you have given me *I have given them*, so that they may be one, as we are one, I in them and you in me, that they may become completely one, so that the world may know that you have sent me and have loved them even as you have loved me. Father, I desire that those also, whom you have given me, may be with me where I am, to see my glory, which you have given me because you loved me before the foundation of the world.[11]

Missing the Glory

You may be asking, "How can you say God shares his glory when the Bible says God cannot share his glory with another?" **This is a good question, and one that gets raised when we talk about the arts, about Mary, and about the saints.** In fact, this text from Isaiah 48 has been used by Protestants for centuries to support a "puritanical" force in the church. Often a verse is taken out of context to prove a point. Let's look at that phrase in context:

> Because I know that you are obstinate, and your neck is an iron sinew and your forehead brass, I declared them to you from of old, before they came to pass I announced them to you, lest you should say, 'My idol did them, my graven image and my molten image commanded them.' "You have heard; now see all this; and will you not declare it? From this time forth I make you hear new things, hidden things which you have not known. They are created now, not long ago; before today you

---

11 John 17:22-24 NRSVA. Emphasis mine.

MARY

have never heard of them, lest you should say, 'Behold, I knew them.' You have never heard, you have never known, from of old your ear has not been opened. For I knew that you would deal very treacherously, and that from birth you were called a rebel. "For my name's sake

I defer my anger, for the sake of my praise I restrain it for you, that I may not cut you off. Behold, I have refined you, but not like silver; I have tried you in the furnace of affliction. For my own sake, for my own sake, I do it, for how should my name be profaned? My glory I will not give to another.[12]

Isaiah 48 talks about the making and creating of idols. And specifically, carved wooden images and metal ones made with a mold. A few chapters earlier, God actually says he is going to put his glory on Israel, and a few chapters later he says that the glory of God will cover the earth. But here, rightly so, God cannot share his glory with an idol. Idols do not reveal God's glory—they are not a manifestation of his presence. But even in the Old Covenant, God does reveal his presence within the people of Israel, and promised that this presence would one day be inside their hearts.

In Romans chapter 1, the connection is made between a hard heart that has rejected God and the worship of idols. When a person rejects God and turns to idols the glory cannot flow. Worse than making idols is what happens to the heart that rejects the Glory of God.

Claiming to be wise, they became fools, and exchanged the glory of the immortal God for images resembling mortal man or birds or animals or reptiles. Therefore God gave them up in the lusts of their hearts to impurity, to the dishonoring of their bodies among themselves, because they exchanged the truth

---

12   Isaiah 48:4-11.

about God for a lie and worshiped and served the creature rather than the Creator, who is blessed for ever! Amen. For this reason God gave them up to dishonorable passions. Their women exchanged natural relations for unnatural, and the men likewise gave up natural relations with women and were consumed with passion for one another, men committing shameless acts with men and receiving in their own persons the due penalty for their error. And since they did not see fit to acknowledge God, God gave them up to a base mind and to improper conduct. They were filled with all manner of wickedness, evil, covetousness, malice. Full of envy, murder, strife, deceit, malignity, they are gossips, slanderers, haters of God, insolent, haughty, boastful, inventors of evil, disobedient to parents, foolish, faithless, heartless, ruthless. Though they know God's decree that those who do such things deserve to die, they not only do them but approve those who practice them.[13]

Idolatry in the New Covenant is not about idols made of wood, stone, or bronze. **Idolatry is about rejection of the Glory that is intended to dwell within you.** It is also the rejecting of God's glory in other believers. This is why we must honor those who we encounter, and those who have gone before us. They are glory-bearers. Like everything else in the New Covenant the stakes are much higher. Rejection of the dynamic charismatic reality of God's action in people has terrible consequences.

Ultimately, idolatry is choosing to reject the Glory of God. And often this rejection begins when we take offense at circumstances or people that God may have been using. Whenever we reject the glory, we begin to go down the road to idolatry.

---

13   Romans 1:22-32.

MARY

A great example of this happened in my home, New England. During the 1730s God began to move mightily across the American Colonies. This movement crystallized in the ministry of Jonathan Edwards, and increased under the ministry of George Whitefield. Throughout North America, thousands of men and women experienced what became known as the "Great Awakening." Sadly, the established Congregational Churches throughout New England resisted and rejected this move of God and became known as the "Old Lights." Those who experienced the revival were called "New Lights." Eventually the New Lights formed new churches, and largely became Presbyterians. And the Old Lights largely rejected the Holy Spirit—and formed the Unitarian church. Across New England the original Puritan churches are all members of the Unitarian-Universalist Association, a denomination that rejects orthodox Christianity, the Holy Spirit, and elevates human reason to the place of the divine. It's a chilling testimony to what happens when we reject the glory.

When we reject the glory, we are rejecting a part of God's Person, Presence, or Power. And if we make that a habit, that becomes resisting the Holy Spirit. It is serious business. It should fill us with holy fear.

Embracing or rejecting God's glory determines your direction. And your internal direction will determine your creative expression. Without the glory you are an idolater. It's not about statues or pictures, its about Presence. It's also all about people.

C. S. Lewis captured the essence of God's plan for us at the end of his lecture, "The Weight of Glory."

> It is a serious thing to live in a society of possible gods and goddesses, to remember that the dullest and most

uninteresting person you can talk to may one day be a creature which, if you saw it now, you would be strongly tempted to worship, or else a horror and a corruption such as you now meet, if at all, only in a nightmare. All day long we are, in some degree, helping each other to one or other of these destinations. It is in the light of these overwhelming possibilities, it is with the awe and the circumspection proper to them, that we should conduct all our dealings with one another, all friendships, all loves, all play, all politics. There are no ordinary people. You have never talked to a mere mortal. Nations, cultures, arts, civilizations—these are mortal, and their life is to ours as the life of a gnat. But it is immortals whom we joke with, work with, marry, snub, and exploit—immortal horrors or everlasting splendors. This does not mean that we are to be perpetually solemn. We must play. But our merriment must be of that kind (and it is, in fact, the merriest kind) which exists between people who have, from the outset, taken each other seriously—no flippancy, no superiority, no presumption. And our charity must be a real and costly love, with deep feeling for the sins in spite of which we love the sinner—no mere tolerance, or indulgence which parodies love as flippancy parodies merriment. Next to the Blessed Sacrament itself, your neighbour is the holiest object presented to your senses. If he is your Christian neighbour, he is holy in almost the same way, for in him also Christ vere latitat—the glorifier and the glorified, Glory Himself, is truly hidden.[14]

We are now going to go back to the story of Mary, and how God through history makes the glory increase.

---

[14] Lewis, C. S. (2009-06-03). Weight of Glory (Collected Letters of C.S. Lewis) (pp. 46-47). HarperCollins. Kindle Edition.

MARY

FOUR

THEME AND VARIATIONS

The first eleven chapters of Genesis are simply amazing. When God inspired the Bible He must have known that many folks would pick up the Bible and not get past the first few pages before losing interest. In the first eight pages or so, all the themes in Scripture can be found. As I stated earlier, the mention of a woman having a child that overcomes the Serpent is found in the Genesis 3:15. In my earlier books I have described this as kind of a tapestry—every thread is laid down at the beginning. The threads re-emerge in other places, and we will see later that all the threads re-appear in the Book of Revelation.

Before we can talk about Mary, we need to talk about the thread that begins in Genesis 3:15. God said he would put enmity between the Serpent and the woman, and that her child would be wounded by the serpent, but the child would crush the serpent's head. In musical terms, this is the introduction of a theme.

In a symphony the composer introduces a musical idea, and it is called a "theme." Then the theme is developed in various ways. Sometimes this development is called "theme and variations." The composer continues to revisit the main form of the theme, and then takes it apart, highlights aspects of it, and changes bits. The composer is trying to get all he can from that little musical idea.

The Bible does the same thing with the Woman/Child theme. It is one of the central themes of Scripture, possibly second only to theme of Marriage. And this "theme and variations" sets the stage for our study of Mary.

Mighty Mothers of God

Whenever God needed a new creative solution for a problem, He used a woman. There are notes of various themes that appear and disappear in each account, so no two are exactly alike. Then in the gospel of Luke, all the themes emerge together to birth the New Covenant.

The first notes of this symphony appear in the book of Genesis. Eve's story is one of a dark minor key, and she is the one who introduces death to the world—even though her name means "Mother of all Living."[15] The dissonant notes of her fall, leading to the birth of a son who commits the first murder begin a deep resonant darkness that will be overcome successively by all the births that follow. This minor beginning in death is going to be overcome by the major chords of life.

Sarah

The first woman to introduce the theme of life in the midst of death is Sarah.[16] Through the word of an angel she is told she will give birth to a son at the age of 90. But Sarah is at the beginning of our symphony, so her response is more like Eve than Mary. She is a variation on the failure of Eve. She laughs at the angel in disbelief. God in the end has the last laugh and names the baby Isaac ("Isaac" means laughter).

---

15   Genesis 3:20.

16   Genesis 21:1-7.

Rebekah

In the next generation, Rebekah the noble wife of Isaac appears. She too is barren, and only gives birth in answer to the prayer made by Isaac in Genesis 25:21. And she overcame death by receiving a "double portion." Rebekah was the mother of Jacob and Esau.

Rachel

In the next generation we have another repeat of the mingling of the theme of death and the theme of life. Rachel is Jacob's first love. Because the deceit of her father, Jacob is tricked into marrying Leah, her sister. And Leah turns out to be a good wife and prolific mother. After finally marrying Jacob, Rachel discovers she is infertile. The once favored love is now the wife of shame. She eventually cries out to God and God removes her shame by giving her a son, Joseph.

Samson

In Judges we find Israel in deep trouble and in need of a national savior. We are not given the name of the woman, but once again we find a barren woman and her husband seeking God for a child.

> And there was a certain man of Zorah, of the tribe of the Danites, whose name was Manoah; and his wife was barren and had no children. And the angel of the LORD appeared to the woman and said to her, "Behold, you are barren and have no children; but you shall conceive and bear a son. Therefore beware, and drink no wine or strong drink, and eat nothing unclean, for lo, you shall conceive and bear a son. No razor shall come upon his head, for the boy shall be a Nazirite to God from birth; and he shall begin to deliver Israel from the hand of the Philistines." Then the woman came and told her husband, "A man of God came to me, and his countenance was like the countenance of the angel of God, very terrible; I did not ask him whence he was, and he did not tell me his name; but he said to me, 'Behold, you shall conceive and bear

a son; so then drink no wine or strong drink, and eat nothing unclean, for the boy shall be a Nazirite to God from birth to the day of his death.'"[17]

As you can see, this story anticipates the story of Mary and Gabriel. For the first time this symphony is not echoing the negative sounds of Eve, but the hopeful sounds of life in the New Covenant. It is a new variation and a shift from minor to major.

> And the woman bore a son, and called his name Samson; and the boy grew, and the LORD blessed him. And the Spirit of the LORD began to stir him in Mahaneh-dan, between Zorah and Eshta-ol. —Judges 14:24

Hannah

Of all the miraculous births, the one that most prefigures Mary is Hannah. Hannah is one of the most poignant characters in the Bible.

Again we meet a barren woman in a polygamous society. Her husband's other wife abuses her, and she becomes desperate. On a trip to the Tabernacle, Hannah cries out to the Lord so intensely that she no longer can even utter a sound. The unrighteous priest Eli chastises her for drunkenness until he learns of her situation. Then he prophesies over her and she gives birth to Samuel. This is the last miraculous birth in the Old Testament and Luke purposely links it to Mary. Mary's song in Luke 1 is largely based on the form and structure of Hannah's song in I Samuel 2:1-10:

---

17 Judges 13:2-7.

THEME AND VARIATIONS

"My heart exults in the Lord;
   my strength is exalted in my God.
My mouth derides my enemies,
   because I rejoice in your salvation.

"There is no Holy One like you, O Lord,
   nor any Rock like you, our God.
For you are a God of knowledge
   and by you our actions are weighed.
The bows of the mighty are broken,
   but the feeble gird on strength.
Those who were full now search for bread,
   but those who were hungry are well fed.
The barren woman has borne sevenfold,
   but she who has many children is forlorn.
Both the poor and the rich are of your making;
   you bring low and you also exalt.
You raise up the poor from the dust,
   and lift the needy from the ash heap.
You make them sit with the rulers
   and inherit a place of honour.
For the pillars of the earth are yours
   and on them you have set the world.

"He will guard the feet of his faithful ones;
   but the wicked shall be cut off in darkness;
   for not by might shall a man prevail.
The adversaries of the Lord shall be broken to pieces;
   against them he will thunder in heaven.
The Lord will judge the ends of the earth;
   he will give strength to his king,
   and exalt the power of his anointed."

MARY

Elizabeth

The births of John and Jesus echo elements of all the previous stories. Elizabeth is a barren woman in advanced age. She also lives under the shame of infertility. At the birth of her child she declares that her reproach is taken away.

All of these stories follow a similar plot: Israel is in a moment of extreme need. Desperate women appear who personify Israel's need. God meets the need of the desperate women by helping them conceive and give birth to a baby.

The solution to the problem is always the birth of a baby.

God uses people to accomplish his purposes. God always uses people to display his Person, Presence, and Power. In this sense, people become sacraments—an outward sign of God's invisible grace.

All of these six women foreshadow Mary's blessedness. Mary was the seventh in an amazing parade of women. God was repeating the theme introduced in Genesis 3. Eve gave us accursedness. These righteous women in increasing measure are releasing blessedness. The curse is overcome through becoming "mothers of the living."

I think we need to also point out that the Bible honors the women and their role. Especially in the case of Hannah and the mother of Samson, these woman took great steps of faith. Several of them acted righteously in unjust cultural structures. They prophetically embodied their nation. A part of this theme of honoring women is being fruitful and multiplication.

Every creative act is an act of giving birth.

THEME AND VARIATIONS

Every creative person has moments of extreme need. Sometimes you feel like you are barren, with no life in you. How does God create out of those barren places? God gives life to dry places by speaking a word.

This metaphor of birth and life is central to Scripture, and central to Mary's story. Now let's look at how this symphony explodes into the New Covenant.

MARY

FIVE

GOD-BEARER

"My name is Daphne," said the muscular young man wearing eyeliner and women's earrings. Like so many of the young people I encountered when we ran a prayer ministry in Boston, Daphne didn't know who he was. And as I talked with him, he wasn't interested in embracing what God said about him. In our conversation I discovered that he was living in *Rosie's Place*, a homeless shelter for abused women. The staff allowed this because he self-identified as female. To be a man for Daphne meant back to living on the street. I quote my friend Kaye Gauder a lot—the culture is screaming.

Our world is asking two questions: **Do I have value, and where do I belong?** There are millions of people in our world today who do not believe they have value, and because of this, they are not sure who they are. This insecurity leads people to all kinds of crazy lifestyle choices as they try to deal with the pain of not knowing who they are—and why they are here.

It is all about identity.

Two Realities

The New Covenant really is new. It's not just the old one with jazzy music. This covenant is about two core realities: God becoming flesh and dwelling with us and Human Beings becoming the living dwelling place of God by the Holy Spirit. It's about where you belong and who you are. This is why Paul called the Corinthian believers

MARY

"temples of the Holy Spirit."[18] The core of this new reality is to bear the glory of God and receive the grace of God.

Before Pentecost, and after Bezalel, there is only one person who physically became a dwelling place for God. That person was Mary.

She is the first person to know the reality of "Christ in you, the hope of glory."[19] Her story is the story of a woman who receives an identity defined by God. By watching her story unfold, we can learn a lot about our own identity. Mary's story begins when God names her through the voice of an angel. It continues with her response, her growth, and ultimately who she became in God.

Because Mary is never raised above creation, her story and its promises become ours. Mary becomes a creator in the image of the Creator, and what she creates redeems the world.

In Mary God decided to do something completely different. He decided to choose a human being to come into the fellowship of the godhead and take the risk of involving a creature in the redemption of creation.

From the little windows into Mary's life the gospels give us, it is clear that Mary herself did not comprehend her identity or understand this mission. And because of her limited perspective, Mary was greatly troubled.

You might be troubled too. Before we go too much further, I want to establish two ground rules for how we talk about Mary:

---

18   I Corinthians 6:19.

19   Colossians 1:27.

Since the early church all conversations concerning Mary have centered on Jesus and the Incarnation. **You cannot say things about Mary unless they say something about Jesus.** As one ancient said, "Mary is like the moon, her glory comes from the Son."

The other ground rule relates to this. **We cannot say something about Mary that in turn does not say something about us.** In this sense, Mary as a created being is "Queen of the Prophets." Her entire life and experience is one of forerunner. She should embody all that is promised to us as believers in the New Covenant.

Throughout this book I am going to take those two ideas and attempt to apply them. Mary's story reveals something about Jesus, and also reveals something about us.

God Perspective

When God pulls back the veil and we begin to see his perspective, we are suddenly frightened. We are frightened by who we are, and who we possibly can become. And most frightening of all—how far below this reality we choose to live. God has so much for every human being, and yet it is easier to muck around in sin and limited potential. Although Daphne is an extreme case, his is the identity crisis that many feel to a certain degree. We don't live up to all we are made to be.

Mary is especially important in this age of identity crisis. It may explain the surge in Marian devotion from Catholics and non-Catholics alike. And Mary is especially important to artists and culture shapers because no person in history actually made the Word flesh the way Mary did.

All generations have called her blessed. And even as the old paganism began to crumble and fade away in the face of growing light, the

MARY

church took the risk and began to look at Mary. In this post-pagan environment they gave Mary a title: *Theotokos*. God-bearer.

God messed with space and time and now God has a Mom.

The word became flesh and one person silently suffered. One *woman* suffered. One woman felt God kick her in the gut. When Jesus felt compassion for the crowds, the Greek says he felt it in the "guts." Mary felt it first.

One woman felt the nausea of pregnancy when God became a man. One woman felt the discomfort as the Son of God grew within her. One woman felt pain and suffered as the labor began that introduced God to the world. And long before blood and water flowed from the side of Christ on the cross, Mary's water broke and blood flowed as the Son of God announced his arrival to the world with a baby's cry. That sound changed the world and Mary forever.

Pay attention to the blood and water. It is a critical detail in the story of Mary. We are going to keep coming back to it again and again.

Every creative act is an act of giving birth and making the Word flesh. And every creative act is the opportunity to walk into the true identity God created for you. You were created to be a little less than God, seated with Christ in heavenly places.[20]

There are hints in the New Testament that Mary was the living version of the Ark made by Bezalel. In this sense, Mary is the Ark made flesh. We will look at this more closely in a later chapter, but the New Covenant begins with a person, not a golden box. God's kingdom is not going to have one throne, but billions who represent his rule and reign on the earth. And Mary was the first.

---

20 Psalm 8:5, NLT and the Hebrew, Ephesians 2:6.

Mary contains the fulfillment of all the promises inside the ark. She holds the Bread of Life, the Fulfillment of the Law and the Prophets and the Great High Priest in the Order of Melchizedek.

David cried out that he could create a resting place on earth for God, but that prayer really never was answered until the New Covenant. Mary is the first *living* resting place of God in the earth, the place where the Glory abides for nine months. God shared his glory with a person.

The plan is that the glory of God would cover the earth like the water covers the sea. The New Covenant way to do this is to create a group of glory-bearers in the earth.

MARY

Glory to you, Lord God of our fathers;
  you are worthy of praise; glory to you.
Glory to you for the radiance of your holy Name;
  we will praise you and highly exalt you for ever.
Glory to you in the splendor of your temple;
  on the throne of your majesty, glory to you.
Glory to you, seated between the Cherubim;
  we will praise you and highly exalt you for ever.
Glory to you, beholding the depths;
  in the high vault of heaven, glory to you.
Glory to you, Father, Son, and Holy Spirit;
  we will praise you and highly exalt you for ever.

—The Song of the Three Young Men in the Fiery Furnace

SIX

GRACE

In the sixth month the angel Gabriel was sent from God to a city of Galilee named Nazareth, to a virgin betrothed to a man whose name was Joseph, of the house of David; and the virgin's name was Mary.

And he came to her and said, "Hail, full of grace, the Lord is with you!" But she was greatly troubled at the saying, and considered in her mind what sort of greeting this might be.

And the angel said to her, "Do not be afraid, Mary, for you have found favor with God. And behold, you will conceive in your womb and bear a son, and you shall call his name Jesus. He will be great, and will be called the Son of the Most High; and the Lord God will give to him the throne of his father David, and he will reign over the house of Jacob for ever; and of his kingdom there will be no end."

And Mary said to the angel, "How shall this be, since I have no husband?" And the angel said to her, "The Holy Spirit will come upon you, and the power of the Most High will overshadow you; therefore the child to be born will be called holy, the Son of God. And behold, your kinswoman Elizabeth in her old age has also conceived a son; and this is the sixth month with her who was called barren. For with God nothing will be impossible."

And Mary said, "Behold, I am the handmaid of the Lord; let it be to me according to your word." And the angel departed from her.[21]

---

21 Luke 1:26-38.

MARY

Mary did not start out believing she had an amazing call from God. It took a moment with an angel, a moment that interrupted her day. It was a moment that would interrupt her life. From the few details we know, it looks like Mary was intent on planning her wedding. She was going to have a good life with Joseph. It was going to be like many other lives—marriage, family, grandchildren, and a family business.

But then there was an angel.

There was nothing wrong or second-rate in Mary's plans for her own future. They were good plans. But then an angel appeared and Mary discovered she was about to be a partaker of the glory.

I love Luke's gospel because of the little details. Luke begins by telling us when it happened, "in the sixth month." This is a little reminder that these are real events. The events happened in real time and space. Mary isn't a "jim-crack mother goddess" created by a syncretizing force in the early church.[22] Here, in the month before Passover, the Angel Gabriel visits a real place and delivers a real message to a real girl who is getting ready for her real wedding.

God sends an angel to insert himself into history, and into a few life stories. Remember, whenever we encounter the glory, we encounter a piece of God's identity. Whenever we encounter the glory we also get a revelation of our own identity as a bonus.

---

22 This term was coined by Dr. Rachel Fulton Brown in her lecture, "Mary in the Scriptures: The Unexpurgated Tradition," part of the Theotokos Lectures in Theology 2014, Marquette University, Milwaukee, Wisconsin.

Let me say that again:

The Glory reveals God's Identity, and in the Glory we discover our true identity.

Gabriel is about to tell Mary who she is.

Fountain of Grace

In Luke 1:28 Gabriel appears and says "He kecharitomene!" Modern Bibles have translated this "highly favored" or "Favored one." This is why knowing about the original languages really is helpful. When you study the Greek, this little phrase is packed with information. The Greek forms a word picture. It tells us a lot about Mary, and a lot about grace.

"Kecharitomene" needs to be pulled apart. The big word for this is "parsed."

The first two letters, the "ke-" prefix, indicate the verb tense. In this case we are looking at the perfect tense. My Greek professor, Dr. Bob Lyon at Asbury, always told us to "pay attention to the kappa" in a word. That meant there was a lot more going on in that phrase than met the eye. This tense, a tense that doesn't exist in English, indicates that something happened in the past, continues in the present, and carries on into the future. It indicates a timeless eternal reality in one word.

The root of this word is "charis." It is the word for grace and gift. It is the root of our English words "charismatic" and "charisma."

The suffix "mene" fills out the title. It can mean full, fullness, or overflowing.

MARY

Put it all together and this is what Gabriel said to the young girl. "Hail you who have been overflowing with grace, who is full of grace now, and who will be full of grace in the future." Another way to put it: "Hail overflowing fountain of grace."[23]

That is a pretty big title for anyone to receive. I guess it is no surprise that Mary was deeply troubled. This is the first time that we get a glimpse into her true identity.

And throughout this encounter, Mary is repeatedly told not to be afraid. Do not be afraid because you have found favor with God. Favor with God is what we call grace. Favor with God is full of blessing, but it is also full of responsibility.

Mary is full of grace, first to experience this miraculous birth, but she is also full of grace to receive the message. And she will be full of grace to carry the child in her body. She will be full of grace to greet the Magi and receive their gifts, and she will be full of grace to become a political refugee in Egypt, and she will be full of grace when she returns to Nazareth. She will be full of grace as she spends her life living with the raised eyebrows of the women in her village, the women who know that something odd happened in her pregnancy with Jesus. She will be full of grace when she loses her son on a pilgrimage to Jerusalem, and we will see her full of grace throughout her son's life and death. It will take supernatural help to do what she is going to do.

So we have looked at what this title tells us about Mary. Now let's talk about what it says concerning grace.

---

23 This description of Mary parallels the description of Bezalel in Exodus 31:1-2. The Hebrew verb tense there indicates Bezalel was also like a fountain overflowing with the Holy Spirit.

Dynamic Grace

Already you can see that grace is not static in Mary's situation. Grace is dynamic. Even in this initial encounter, grace is flowing. The angel points out that Mary has received grace, and that more grace is about to be poured out.

> The Holy Spirit will come upon you and the Power of the Most High will overshadow you; therefore the child to be born will be called Holy, the Son of God.[24]

Grace is not merely a legal state, "the unmerited favor of God" that you come into and never see flow or move. Grace is dynamic. It increases, decreases, and moves. Just like the glory is not an idea, but a thing, so is grace. Grace has substance. The dynamic flow of grace is an abundant source of creativity. In fact, all creative output is a reflection of grace.

And grace has a relationship to the glory. Grace cannot be separated from God's Person, Presence, and Power. Whenever we experience grace, we also experience a part of God's identity.

From this brief encounter between Mary and Gabriel we can draw a few conclusions.
- Grace is the outworking of the power of God.
- Grace is the manifestation of the Holy Spirit.
- Grace is another aspect of God's self-manifestation.

Grace in many ways is like God's glory. In fact, I think it is hard to separate the two.

---

24 Luke 1:35.

And whenever grace is in action, something changes. In this case, the lives of Mary and Joseph are changed. And ultimately, human history will be changed. Grace is the practical application of God's goodness. God is good, his love endures for ever. Whenever this goodness touches the created realm, something changes for the good. And as we will see later, Mary's calling is to be a fountain of grace and that means she will initiate change.

Three Kinds of Grace

Throughout history, many teachers have identified three kinds of grace in the life of the believer. And we can see all three types of grace present in the life of Mary. These types of grace are Preceding, Justifying, and Sanctifying grace.

Preceding grace is the grace that goes before you.[25] One of the Hebrew names for God is "YHWH-Shammah." This is the "Lord who is there." No matter what, God has always gone before you. God knows the end from the beginning, and when you get there you suddenly see God's handprints on everything. It's the grace that prepares you to have an encounter with God. It is the grace that makes you hungry and willing to come to God. It is the grace that leads to a change of heart and mind. This old hymn by an unknown poet describes the reality of preceding grace.

> I sought the Lord, and afterward I knew
> He moved my soul, to seek Him, seeking me.
> It was not I that found, O Saviour true.
> No, I was found of thee.

---

25   John Wesley and the Council of Trent referred to this type of grace as "Prevenient" or "Preventing" grace. Both of these terms are confusing to contemporary readers. After consulting with noted Wesley scholar, Dr. Ken Collins, I have settled on the term "preceding."

GRACE

Mary found herself found by God. This was the grace in her life that prepared her for the day when Gabriel greeted her.

The second kind of grace is Justifying grace. This is the grace we experience at the moment of conversion. It is the moment when God calls us by name and we hear his voice. It is the moment we say "Yes" to God. It is the moment when Thomas said "my Lord and my God" and the moment when we confess with our mouth "Jesus is Lord" and believe in our heart God raised him from the dead. It is the grace of baptism. This is the grace that saves and transforms. It is the moment when Wesley's heart was strangely warmed. It is the moment when Francis answered the call to leave father and mother. **This is the saving action of the Holy Spirit.**

Mary's justification came in the dramatic moment when she said "let it be to me according to your word." Mary's "yes" made it possible for all of us to say "yes" to Jesus. Again we see Mary going ahead of us, supernaturally receiving and acting on a grace that is part of a yet to be revealed covenant. Mary, by faith, accessed something that would not be available to others for at least three decades.

There is a beautiful orthodox hymn that expresses this moment.

> You have beheld the King in his beauty,
> Mary, daughter of Israel.
> You have made answer for the creation
> To the redeeming will of God.
> Light, fire and life, divine and immortal,
> Joined to our nature you have brought forth,
> That to the glory of God the Father,
> Heaven and earth might be restored.[26]

---

26 Orthodox hymn translated by West Malling. *Celebrating Common Prayer*, 1995. p. 267.

MARY

And finally, there is the most wonderful grace of all: Sanctifying grace. This is the grace of God that makes us holy.

Sanctifying grace begins the moment after we know that we have been redeemed and received into the company of the elect. It is the beginning of our history in God. Sanctification never ends. The process begins with the Holy Spirit highlighting the sinful bits and giving us the ability to be transformed. But sanctification is much more than being free from sin. Sanctification continues with cleansing and healing. In fullness, Sanctification is the wonderful call to endless becoming. Becoming holy is becoming more and more the real you, the you that God truly created you to be. Sanctification is discovering your true identity and living it out. It is the transformation of the inner life. The inner life determines one's creative output.

And in Mary's life we will see how this grace begins to express itself as she struggles to discover what it means to be a fountain of grace.

All three types of grace are present in this first moment between Mary and Gabriel. Grace went before Mary and prepared the way. Preceding grace was present in her lineage as a descendant of David, in her betrothal to Joseph, and even in the historic context she was born into. Justifying grace filled Mary and made it possible for her to say yes and respond to the favor of God. Sanctifying grace will manifest in the physical conception of Jesus when the Word will become flesh—and the word of grace will manifest in her body.

This is the first moment in life when Mary gets a glimpse of her place in God's economy. It is a moment of revelation and fear.

Experiencing Grace

We all have moments when God takes away our blinders and we see for a moment who we are and who we can be. It is the working of God's grace on the inside that motivates and empowers us to become light, fire, and life, divine and immortal. The working of God's grace in our life makes this possible. It was the plan from the beginning.

God wants you to embrace the working of grace. You are more than you think you are, and you can do and be more than you imagine.

> *Jesus, thank you that you are the author of grace. Thank you that you recognized the grace you put into Mary to be your mother. May I embrace the grace that has gone before me, stand in the grace that has saved me, and continue in the grace that is transforming me into an ever-becoming fountain of grace for others. Amen.*

MARY

SEVEN

ARK

In those days Mary arose and went with haste into the hill country, to a city of Judah, and she entered the house of Zechariah and greeted Elizabeth.

And when Elizabeth heard the greeting of Mary, the babe leaped in her womb; and Elizabeth was filled with the Holy Spirit and she exclaimed with a loud cry, "Blessed are you among women, and blessed is the fruit of your womb! And why is this granted me, that the mother of my Lord should come to me? For behold, when the voice of your greeting came to my ears, the babe in my womb leaped for joy. And blessed is she who believed that there would be a fulfilment of what was spoken to her from the Lord."

And Mary remained with her about three months, and returned to her home. —Luke 1:39-56

A Throne in the Earth

God's plan from the beginning was to retake planet earth. God has patiently followed a slow strategy of taking ground. The first physical representation of this takeover was in the Tabernacle of Moses.

The Tabernacle was like an embassy of a foreign nation. Inside an embassy all the laws and customs of the foreign nation are in operation. It is the place where a nation interfaces with a foreign nation. When you entered the Tabernacle, all the rules, laws, and

MARY

customs of the Kingdom of Heaven were supposed to operate. It was supposed to look a little like heaven, and it was supposed to be a physical base of heaven on earth. It was a place of fellowship, worship, and beauty. In the center of the Tabernacle was the tent that contained the Ark of the Covenant.

As an aside, all the items in the Tabernacle were blessed and dedicated to God by being sprinkled with blood. And all the sacrifices, as well as the priests, were washed with water. **Pay attention to the blood and the water.**

In *Bezalel* I proposed that the Ark of the Covenant was a portable throne. The Ark was a place where God's glory resided. It was also the location where the people of Israel obtained mercy. The portable ark was a physical representation of the rule and reign of God in the earth just like a throne in a monarchy represents the rule and reign of the monarch.

If you imagine that the Ark is a throne, then you begin to see a direct connection between what God was doing in the Old Covenant, and what Jesus came to do in establishing a Kingdom. God was establishing a kingdom from the very beginning. First it was symbolized by the throne in the Tabernacle. Then it was established by the one promised to sit upon the throne of David.

Luke is one of my favorite Biblical writers. He is the only Gentile who contributed to the Bible. He brings a fresh perspective, one that looks at the story of Jesus from the perspective of an outsider coming into the community of believers. As a result, Luke pays attention to the poor, the women, and the outsiders who all were touched by Jesus and welcomed into the early church. Luke always brings a lot of details to his narrative.

Because he was a convert, Luke seems to have an exhaustive knowledge of the Greek translation of the Hebrew Bible, the *Septuagint*. Luke's brilliant use of the Bible is similar to the way Shakespeare wove references and allusions to the classics into his plays and poetry. Luke was a traveling companion of Paul, and he must have been well educated in the same way Paul was. There is no proof of this, but I often wonder if Paul and Luke were boyhood friends.

In his gospel, Luke weaves the Ark of the Covenant into the story of Mary and Elizabeth.

In II Samuel the people of Israel have been longing for a savior who would restore their glory. They were looking for someone who would bring back the Ark of the Covenant, lost earlier in I Samuel under the poor leadership of the house of Eli. The Ark was the center of Israel's worship of God. It was the tangible sign that God was the ruler of Israel. When Israel chose a king in the place of God, that throne was not in the center. Saul was a king in place of God. His failure resulted in Israel longing for a king who would be under the rule and reign of God—not a ruler in place of God. That king was David.

The climax of II Samuel 6 is the moment David went and retrieved the Ark from the home of Obed-Edom.

> And it was told King David, "The Lord has blessed the household of Obed-edom and all that belongs to him, because of the ark of God." So David went and brought up the ark of God from the house of Obed-edom to the city of David with rejoicing; and when those who bore the ark of the Lord had gone six paces, he sacrificed an ox and a fatling. And David danced before the Lord with all his might; and David was

MARY

girded with a linen ephod. So David and all the house of Israel brought up the ark of the Lord with shouting, and with the sound of the horn . . . And they brought in the ark of the Lord, and set it in its place, inside the tent which David had pitched for it; and David offered burnt offerings and peace offerings before the Lord. And when David had finished offering the burnt offerings and the peace offerings, he blessed the people in the name of the Lord of hosts, and distributed among all the people, the whole multitude of Israel, both men and women, to each a cake of bread, a portion of meat, and a cake of raisins. Then all the people departed, each to his house.[27]

We do not usually think of Luke as an artist—but he was. Luke artfully takes phrases from the Greek text in II Samuel and puts them into the meeting of Mary and Elizabeth. This is one of those times when reading the original Greek opens your eyes to more in the text. Here is an article from the *Ignatius Catholic Study Bible* that describes in detail how Luke linked Mary to the Ark.

> One tradition that Luke draws upon is from 2 Samuel. He intentionally sets up the subtle but significant parallels between Mary's Visitation with Elizabeth and David's effort to bring the Ark of the Covenant to Jerusalem narrated in 2 Sam 6. When Luke tells us that Mary "arose and went" into the Judean hill country to visit her kinswoman (Lk 1:39), he reminds us of how David "arose and went" into the same region centuries earlier to retrieve the Ark (2 Sam 6:2). Upon Mary's arrival, Elizabeth is struck by the same sense of awe and unworthiness before Mary (Lk 1:43) that David felt standing before the Ark of the Covenant (2 Sam 6:9). Parallels continue as the joy surrounding this great encounter causes the infant John to leap with excitement (Lk 1:41), much

---

27 II Samuel 6:12-15, 17-19.

ARK

as David danced with excitement before the Ark (2 Sam 6:16). Finally, Luke adds that Mary stayed in the "house of Zechariah" for "three months" (Lk 1:40, 56), recalling how the Ark of Covenant was temporarily stationed in the "house of Obed-edom" for a waiting period of "three months" (2 Sam 6:11). Taken together, these parallels show us that Mary now assumes a role in salvation history that was once played by the Ark of the Covenant. Like this golden chest, she is a sacred vessel where the Lord's presence dwells intimately with his people.[28]

You may be saying to yourself, "This sounds like an interesting (or boring!) study, but if Luke was linking Mary to the Ark, why didn't he just say it?"

When you go to the movies you often notice that the musical score will make references to recognizable songs to highlight the image. In a movie it's not unusual to see an image of Big Ben and hear "Rule Britannia" in the background, or in cartoons "Jingle Bells" plays when the character encounters snow or references Christmas. To the original hearers of this gospel, Luke was creating the same sort of allusion. Luke was an artist, he used this literary device to add dimension to the story of Mary and Elizabeth. He was adding a layer of depth. The story of the Ark in II Samuel is the musical score playing behind the story of Mary and Elizabeth. And Luke made another allusion that strengthens the case that he was trying to link Mary to the Ark.

Shout Before the Ark

When you learn Biblical Greek, you are only taught the words that occur repeatedly in the New Testament. The New Testament has a

---

28 Hahn, Scott; Mitch, Curtis (2010-06-14). The Ignatius Catholic Study Bible New Testament (Kindle Locations 8229-8239). Ignatius Press. Kindle Edition.

MARY

limited vocabulary, and you are taught to use reference books when you encounter an unusual term. To a person familiar with the Greek New Testament, a word that is rare or obscure is easy to notice. Luke puts an obscure Greek word into the mouth of Elizabeth when she meets Mary. In Luke 1:42 it says that Elizabeth "exclaimed" when she met Mary. That word is used once in the New Testament, and only 5 times in the entire Greek Bible. At the time of Luke, a person who had knowledge of the Bible would recognize the connection Luke was making.

Elizabeth's exclamation only occurs before the Ark of the Covenant in the Tabernacle of David. It was the shout they raised when the Ark was moved into Jerusalem, and it was the shout that was heard when Solomon moved the Ark into the New Temple. It was the sound of the people in response to the glory of God over the Ark.[29] We should also note that whenever this sound was made, the Glory of God appeared.

Elizabeth, a woman, is representing her tribe, the tribe of Levi. Ironically, she is married to a priest who has been struck dumb from disbelief. Elizabeth is walking into a new role of priest before a new Ark made flesh. Elizabeth is given a voice when her husband is silent. Radically, Elizabeth gets to speak on behalf of man.

In this little scene we are given a glimpse through Luke's New Covenant lens. Gentile Luke sees God entering space and time. All the boundaries based on physical location, sex, tribe, and race are giving way to a New Kingdom in the Holy Spirit. Now God is building a kingdom using people. And Elizabeth greets this new reality with a shout of worship.

---

29   I Chronicles 15:28, 16:4-5, II Chronicles 5:13.

Elizabeth takes on the role of priest before this new Ark in a way her husband never could have in his role as a levitical priest. She represents the tribe of Levi. She greets Mary a descendant of David of the tribe of Judah. Judah was not a priestly tribe but Jesus would become a priest. Hebrews says that Jesus was a priest in the order of Melchizedek. Here we begin the shift from a priesthood in the order of Levi to a new priesthood in the order of Melchizedek. Mary's son will increase. Elizabeth's son will decrease.

This moment ends much like the day Solomon's temple was dedicated. The Glory fills a new physical temple.

In a very real way, God is sharing his glory with Mary. As I pointed out earlier, whenever God reveals his glory, He is revealing something about his Person, Presence, and Power. And that glory is beginning to pour out and touch others.

Luke paints a striking contrast to II Samuel 6 where Uzzah touches the Ark and dies. The Ark contained the Tablets of Law, a covenant of wrath.[30] Whoever touches this improperly dies. Mary's womb contains the Word of Life. So Mary becomes a life bringer. Mary speaks to Elizabeth and John is filled with the Spirit of Life. John leaps, just like David, at the sound of Mary's voice. This New Covenant Ark is the bringer of life. God is revealing himself as the Lord and Giver of Life.

The New Testament will link Mary to the Ark again in Revelation chapter 12. We will look at that passage later.

---

30 Romans 4:15.

MARY

God is birthing a creative revolution, and we see it in this encounter linking Mary and Elizabeth to the history of Israel. And Luke redefines that reference through signs and wonders as the New Covenant is revealed in their presence. God is doing a new thing through two women pushed to the boundaries of faith and belief.

St. Ambrose, in the fifth century, talked about it this way:

> And Mary's arrival and the presence of her Son quickly show their effects: As soon as Elizabeth heard Mary's greeting her child leapt in her womb and she was filled with the Holy Spirit.
>
> But notice the careful choice, the delicate precision, of each word. Elizabeth was the first to hear the voice, but John was the first to feel the grace. The woman, under the laws of nature, heard; but the child under the influence of mystery, leaped for joy.
>
> Elizabeth recognized the arrival of Mary, but the little one recognized the coming of the Lord. The woman saw the Woman, the child perceived the Child. The women speak words of grace; the little ones engage in the mystery of love and mercy for the benefit of their mothers. **And, by a double miracle, the mothers prophesy under the inspiration of their children.**
>
> The child leaped for joy [because] the mother was filled with the Spirit. The mother was not filled before her son, but when the son was filled with the Holy Spirit, then the mother too was filled. John leaped for joy, and the spirit of Mary rejoiced. As John leaped, Elizabeth was filled. We are not told that Mary was filled with the Holy Spirit, but that her spirit rejoiced for

He who was incomprehensible was working within the Mother in a way that is beyond our comprehension.

In short Elizabeth was filled after she conceived. Mary was filled before she conceived.[31]

Making it Practical

Earlier I said everything we say about Mary has to say something about Jesus, and it also has to say something about us.

What does Luke's allusion to the Ark tell us about Jesus? The Old Covenant Ark carried the tablets of Law, a container of Manna, and the staff of Aaron that gave authority to his priesthood. Mary carries in her body the Word made flesh, the Bread of Life, and the High Priest in the Order of Melchizedek. Jesus is the physical, living representation of all the best of the Old Covenant. As Jesus himself said, he came to be the fulfillment of the Law and the Prophets.

What does this say about us? Mary becomes a living Ark, and all this is made possible by the Holy Spirit. This is God's plan from the beginning, to create living thrones throughout the earth who bear his Word in the flesh. Mary is the forerunner. And it is possible because of the Holy Spirit.

You too are called to be a living Ark. The Kingdom is not advanced by establishing big buildings for people to come in and encounter replicas of heaven. The Kingdom is advanced through men and women who are living replicas of heaven. God desires to put his glory and grace in you so that you are a priest, a prophet and a king in the earth. God wants you to be an agent of transformation and shifting in the world. You are called to build the culture of heaven in the earth.

---

31 Ambrose, and Ide M. Ni Riain. *Commentary of Saint Ambrose on the Gospel according to Saint Luke*. Dublin: Halcyon, 2001, p. 35. emphasis mine.

MARY

Are you filled with the Holy Spirit? Have you had a living encounter with the Person, Presence, and Power of God? If you haven't figured it out, the Glory is the Holy Spirit, and the Holy Spirit is Grace. These are not impersonal concepts that we study and think about. These are aspects of a living God who wants to inhabit you just like the Tabernacle.

> *Holy Spirit, I welcome you into my heart that I might be a living Tabernacle, and an Ark of your Presence. Inhabit me and sit upon my life that I might be a throne of your kingdom in the earth.*

In the next chapter we are going to look at Mary in her role of mother, and how that role gives us a model for creativity.

EIGHT

BLESSED

And when Elizabeth heard the greeting of Mary, the babe leaped in her womb; and Elizabeth was filled with the Holy Spirit and she exclaimed with a loud cry, "Blessed are you among women, and blessed is the fruit of your womb! And why is this granted me, that the mother of my Lord should come to me? For behold, when the voice of your greeting came to my ears, the babe in my womb leaped for joy. And blessed is she who believed that there would be a fulfilment of what was spoken to her from the Lord."

Then his mother and his brethren came to him, but they could not reach him for the crowd. And he was told, "Your mother and your brethren are standing outside, desiring to see you." But he said to them, "My mother and my brethren are those who hear the word of God and do it." —Luke 8:19-21

As he said this, a woman in the crowd raised her voice and said to him, "Blessed is the womb that bore you, and the breasts that you sucked!" But he said, "Blessed rather are those who hear the word of God and keep it!" —Luke 11:27-29

Mary wasn't a pod that contained the Son of God.

Maybe that bears repeating.

Mary wasn't a pod that contained the Son of God.

MARY

She wasn't disposable. In fact, the life of Mary is a reminder of how God works through people. Elizabeth cried out to her, "Blessed are you among women, and blessed is the fruit of your womb." Mary herself would declare, "All generations will call me blessed, because the Almighty has done great things for me." And truthfully, aside from Our Lord's command to break bread and share the cup, no text of Scripture has been more accurately repeated and acted out.

Mary's blessedness comes from two things: her ability to hear the word and respond to it. Because Mary heard the word and said "yes" she became the mother of the Messiah. These two aspects also highlight her moments of real humanity. It is at this crossroads that the very human aspects of Mary's personality meet the calling to be the Mother of the Son of God.

Birthing New Things

Mary is the prototype for how God does things in the New Covenant. God does things in natural, yet utterly supernatural ways. As I stated in my book *An Army Arising*, in the New Covenant God is not creating "ex nihilo." That means "out of nothing." God is creating "ex utero." He is birthing things and using people to do it. If you are an artist or creative person, this should make you very excited. You were specifically born and created to function in this New Covenant reality. And the core of this reality honors people and relationships, whether they be souls reborn to eternal life or new expressions of creativity. **Creative reality functions best through honor and relationships.**

In fact, God's way is radically different from the way most earthly leaders operate. God does not use people to accomplish some project or meet some goal and then discard the person when the job is done. God does not "lord over" people like the Gentiles do, as Jesus once said. Once God starts working with a person, that relationship is never intended to end. It is meant to continue. Every person is priceless, and God does not sacrifice people for programs, projects, or politics. God's system is not founded on performance and the people he uses are not expendable. In fact, that attitude of expendability is what motivated the priests to crucify Jesus. It is the idea that some people are "more equal" than others. It is the spirit of Anti-Christ.

This passage from *An Army Arising* bears repeating:

> **Something Out of Nothing**
> Classical theology has a Latin term for this: ex nihilo sui et subiecti—God makes something out of nothing. This idea of ex nihilo, that God speaks and something happens, is one of the central themes of Biblical truth. In the beginning was the WORD. We will see this theme repeated in the Scripture again and again as God speaks. Through prophets, angels, teachers, and ultimately, through his own Son, God speaks.
>
> God is always communicating.
>
> And if God is always communicating, we have to also believe that God is a person, and that God is relational. Ultimately this personal communication reveals that God is Love.
>
> **God Becomes the Word**
> So back to God and the artist. Eventually it became time for the greatest performance art piece of all time. God decided to take on flesh. God decided to become the sermon. God became the living example of all that he had said. How did God do it? By very unnatural, yet completely natural means.
>
> *The Word was spoken, and a virgin conceived.*

MARY

But this conception was not ex nihilo. This creation was the union between the flesh of a person and the word of God.

That human person becomes our model if we are going to completely embrace our destiny as artists. Mary is our model in the creative life.

Co-Laboring with God
Every artist has to co-labor with what is within them. And we have to cooperate with the physical realities of our medium. Along with this, we have to accept the limitations of our own skills and choose to accept our creation. A creative act begins with a germ of an idea, it grows within us, and then it begins to burst forth. Every artist comes to a point where they are not happy until they finish the project they started.

Birthing the Word
Mary encountered the angel Gabriel and Gabriel spoke to her the Word of God. In the speaking, the Holy Spirit began to move in her. When she made the decision, the choice, to embrace the Word and agree with it, her faith activated the Word. At the moment she said, "Let it be to me according to your word" her flesh came into agreement with the Word. At that profound moment the Word was bonded with her DNA and a completely new thing was created. Just like the artist with his or her paints, there was a moment of yielding and then the creative process took over. I imagine Mary, like so many of us creatives, became completely engrossed in her pregnancy. And like the artist, there was a moment of agony where she experienced the pain of childbirth. Only Mary experienced pain when the Word became flesh. Creation caused Mary pain—real physical pain.

An artist experiences agony as the project develops, as the costs mount. Creation requires sacrifice and when it is finished it is embraced by a few but misunderstood and rejected by many. Every creative endeavor is risky. Making the invisible visible is dangerous work. Every act of creativity is an act of Incarnation.

From Bethlehem to Jerusalem Mary learned this. She fled Herod. She saw how the crowds pressed Jesus. She walked with him to the cross. She witnessed the resurrection, and she experienced the first Baptism of the Holy Spirit. Through it all she participated in the new creation. This time it was not ex nihilo—out of nothing, but ex utero—out of the womb.[32]

True Blessedness

Mary's blessedness was not based on any ideal of human motherhood. In fact, the quotes from Luke 8 and 11 at the beginning of this chapter intentionally contrast the "good mother" with true blessedness.

When Mary stood outside and demanded to see Jesus, we get a glimpse of her false identity. She is not a fountain of grace and favor here. She is being the pushy "stage mother." Luke (as well as Matthew and Mark) give us this snapshot of Mary during the middle of the ministry of Jesus. Mary appears outside a place where Jesus is teaching and working miracles. Mary is trying to make a way for herself and the rest of the family. The gospels tell us nothing more than they wanted to see him. It's an odd moment in the gospel narrative, but an opportunity for Jesus to make a point.

Did Mary want to be in the center? Was she trying to get Jesus to come home and fulfill his family duties? Was she hoping to get a piece of the celebrity? We do not know. But Jesus rebukes the crowd, and recalibrates Mary's identity.

---

32 Otto, Christ, *An Army Arising: Why Artists are on the Frontline of the Next Move of God*, p. 51-56.

MARY

> "Who are my mother and brothers? Those who hear the Word of God and keep it."

Mary must have heard the word and been pierced in her heart. It was she who said, "Let it be to me according to your word." It was for this response that all generations would call her blessed. They would not call her blessed for being the ideal mother. Rather, we call her blessed for being the ideal receiver of the word.

Mary is important because she said yes to God. Not because she models an ideal mother. This is a critical distinction, and why Mary serves as a model for every believer.

This moment may have been the low point in the relationship between Mary and Jesus. This was the moment when Mary really needed to let go and allow her son to be the Son of Man. Mary didn't get to see her son that day. Instead she was reminded of why she was blessed. **She became a mother because she received the Word.**

A few chapters later a woman in the crowd cries out, "Blessed is the womb that bore you and the breasts that nursed you." Jesus again corrects the woman. The New Covenant is not based on ideal standards of motherhood and family. The gospel doesn't idolize the human family. This is about a family in relationship to the Father. You cannot be blessed in this family unless you hear the voice of the Father and respond to it.

> "Blessed are those who hear the word of God and keep it."

This is not a diminishment of Mary. Rather, it highlights the core of her blessedness, and how she became one of the pre-eminent figures in the Bible. Mary heard the word, believed it, and responded in faith. She is blessed because she said "yes."

That faith ignited a conception and brought her into a relationship with Elizabeth. All generations have called her blessed because she agreed with the Word becoming flesh in her.

Saying "yes" is the beginning of every act of creation. Those who create hear the word of God and let it become flesh through them. This is the path to blessing—letting the active word come through you to give life to others.

Mary wasn't a pod that bore the Son of God. She was a vessel of honor. Hearing the word of God and keeping it releases a cycle of life that brings honor, blessing, and creativity to others.

And in our next episode Mary's honor will only increase.

MARY

NINE

WOMAN

On the third day there was a marriage at Cana in Galilee, and the mother of Jesus was there; Jesus also was invited to the marriage, with his disciples.

When the wine failed, the mother of Jesus said to him, "They have no wine."

And Jesus said to her, "O woman, what have you to do with me? My hour has not yet come."

His mother said to the servants, "Do whatever he tells you."

Now six stone jars were standing there, for the Jewish rites of purification, each holding twenty or thirty gallons. Jesus said to them, "Fill the jars with water." And they filled them up to the brim. He said to them, "Now draw some out, and take it to the steward of the feast." So they took it. When the steward of the feast tasted the water now become wine, and did not know where it came from (though the servants who had drawn the water knew), the steward of the feast called the bridegroom and said to him, "Every man serves the good wine first; and when men have drunk freely, then the poor wine; but you have kept the good wine until now."

This, the first of his signs, Jesus did at Cana in Galilee, and manifested his glory; and his disciples believed in him.
— John 2:1-11

MARY

John's Gospel is my favorite. As a work of literature it is unparalleled in the small details in the story, and in the larger themes and ideas that you can follow from beginning to end. In many ways, it is a miniature example of the threads you find throughout the entire Bible. John tells his amazing story using a basic knowledge of Greek. In the original language it is like reading profound truth written by Doctor Seuss. *That* is art.

A New Creation

John writes like a poet and echoes the first chapters of the book of Genesis. The Bible begins with "in the beginning God created" and John begins with "In the beginning was the Word." John also breaks up the first two chapters of his gospel into a series of days. John purposefully lays out the first "week" of the ministry of Jesus much like Genesis lays out the first week of the history of the world.

John begins with the Baptism of Jesus—and introduces a primary theme in his gospel, water. Water is going to reappear again and again, and in each case, as in the first chapter, water is linked to Baptism and the Holy Spirit. If you count the days from his baptism, Jesus calls his disciples on the fifth day. Then John skips days six and seven and introduces us to the first act of Jesus' ministry "on the third day."

"On the third day there was a marriage at Cana."

The early Christian community inherited a lot of Jewish symbols and ideas about time and numbers. We see these themes again and again through the New Testament: 40 days and nights, the seven days of creation, and the number three. By the time John wrote his gospel, the church already had linked the resurrection of Jesus to the "third day."

John is no longer looking backward, he is looking forward to another Third Day. This is the day Jesus rose from the dead, and to the Last Day, another Third Day in the Jewish mind: The Day of the Lord. And what happens on that Day? A wedding.

John is telling several stories at once, much like how Luke was overlapping stories in his gospel. John is telling us the story of a New Creation. John is telling us the story of a New Covenant. And John is also telling us the Big Story of the Bible. The Bible is the Story of Father looking for a Bride for his Son. The Bible begins with a Wedding in a garden. It ends with a wedding between the Bride and the Lamb. In the middle is the graphic story of a honeymoon, the story of a poor woman redeemed through marriage, and the story of a prophet who marries a prostitute. And here, we have the beginning of the ministry of Jesus, drawing all these themes together. Marriage is the major story of the Bible. And marriage is at the beginning of John's gospel. John introduces us to the mother of Jesus at a wedding.

A New Eve

John never calls Mary by name. When Jesus speaks to her, he calls her "Woman." And when John references her, she is always the Mother of Jesus. Often I have heard speakers say Jesus called Mary "woman" because it was an ancient term of respect. There is no evidence in ancient writing to support this. Rather, it is a literary device. John is once again making reference to Genesis. As I pointed out earlier, Mary is the culmination of a series of mighty women who are called to bring life to the world and undo Eve's act of bringing death. John is linking Mary to Eve. She is the New Woman, just as Jesus is the New Man.

MARY

We know John had a school of disciples, and we have some of the writings of those who were discipled by him. And we also have the writings of those who were discipled by John's disciples. One of John's spiritual "sons" was Justin Martyr. He is the first to write about Mary and her role as a new Eve in 155:

> ... and that [Jesus] became man by the Virgin, in order that the disobedience which proceeded from the serpent might receive its destruction in the same manner in which it derived its origin.
>
> For Eve, who was a virgin and undefiled, having conceived the word of the serpent, brought forth disobedience and death. But the Virgin Mary received faith and joy, when the angel Gabriel announced the good tidings to her that the Spirit of the Lord would come upon her, and the power of the Highest would overshadow her: wherefore also the Holy Thing begotten of her is the Son of God; and she replied, 'Be it unto me according to thy word.'[33]

Mary plays an interesting part in the Wedding at Cana. In fact, she is the one who moves the plot along. She is the one who notices that there is no wine. As we said before, creativity begins with pointing out what is broken or missing. Mary is taking on a creative role. She begins with what is broken or missing, and is going to birth a creative shalom solution. There is no wine.

Mary Speaks

The Bible as a whole records very few words from Mary. I recently had dinner with a theologian who challenged me about writing this book. Correctly, he pointed out that the Q'uran contains more text

---

33   Justin Martyr, *Dialogue with Trypho*, Chapter C. Christian Classics Ethereal Library, CCEL.org.

about Mary than the New Testament. When you read books about Mary and the Bible, the first chapter is always about how little the Bible says about her compared to the amount of art, literature, and devotion she has inspired. But here we have two phrases from the mouth of Mary: "They have no wine" and "Do whatever He tells you."

Mary points out the problem, and then gives us the solution.

In the world of Orthodox icons, there are many rules about how to depict Mary in visual form. According to tradition, Mary is not to appear alone. Jesus must always be with her in the picture. There are two primary styles of icons used to portray Mary. Mary is often shown in a "lovingkindness" pose, where her cheek and the cheek of Jesus touch, and they are shown in a deep expression of love for each other. This icon is designed to draw the viewer into the "lovingkindness of God" expressed in this intimate relationship. The second primary form is called "Hodegetria." This type of icon depicts Mary pointing to her Son. It is a reminder to us that Mary's primary mission was to bring her Son to the World, and our primary calling is to follow her example by pointing to Jesus as well.

Here at Cana, Mary points us to her Son.

John builds the drama, and Jesus resists his mother.

"Woman, it is not time," he tells her.

Remember that John is echoing the beginning of Genesis. John mirrors the story of temptation. Mary is going to undo Eve's choice, and she is going turn to the new Adam. And unlike the first Adam, Jesus resists the temptation. John puts this wedding at the place where the other gospels send Jesus into the wilderness to be tempted by

MARY

Satan. John is emphasizing that this is a test. Mary, in a way that only a Jewish mother could do, "puts the Lord God to the test" at a wedding.

And Jesus responds to his mother.

There are no details of what happened next. We don't have facial expressions or a film record. But we do have a persistent woman determined to see the glory that has been hidden inside her body get released for all the world to see. Mary wants the glory to manifest. Maybe the persistent widow that Jesus talked about in the Sermon on the Mount was the persistent widow he knew and loved. Maybe she was his own Mother?

At the wedding at Cana all of the expected roles get shaken. Jesus the guest becomes the host. Jesus, the Son of God becomes the Bridegroom. Mary the powerless widow becomes the powerful mover of the hand of God. A widow becomes the Bride. The God in the flesh who hears the cry of the widow hears the cry of his mother, and Jesus relents.

Mary becomes the initiator of the first miracle.

God shared his glory with this woman and she understood that her words, her faith, and her compassion could cause her son make wine out of water.

John's gospel doesn't include a birth narrative, but here we see the birth of the ministry of Jesus. Just as water and blood flow in birth, water and wine flow at this birth. We will see water and blood later in this gospel, but here it is water and wine. This is a metaphor first used by Jacob in Genesis 49:11, when he called wine the "blood of the grape." Mary had been carrying a promise since the birth of Jesus, and throughout her life this promise was carried just like a child in her womb. The blood and water that was released in Bethlehem gets transformed. This miracle is Mary's "second birth" when her child is revealed as the Son of the Most High.

Notice Mary never tells Jesus what to do. She tells the others to listen to Jesus, and do what he tells them. It was her undoing of Eve's choice that allowed Mary to unlock heaven. And it was the servants' listening and obeying that completed the miracle. This is a very different dynamic than we usually see in prayer. Her unlocking released at least 240 gallons of wine! Now that's a creative miracle.

This was the first of the signs that Jesus performed and manifested his glory. Once again, Mary becomes the partaker and sharer of glory. And once again, we see a glimpse into the character of God. We have a God who loves life, loves marriage and family, and who loves celebration. The text also lets us know God has a pretty good taste in wine! And because of this, the disciples believed in Jesus. I guess the disciples liked wine too.

Winemaking
When we listen to God, and do what he tells us we are guaranteed two things. First, we are going to see whatever it is that God wants to release through us. Second, someone is going to believe. And many times we are the first who overcome unbelief, and then others follow.

Earlier we talked about how things shifted in the New Covenant. In this new thing, God is not displaying his glory through thunder, lightning, or clouds. God is revealing his glory through gallons and gallons of wine. In this new thing, we can drink the Glory. We can take in the Presence and we can be inebriated in grace. And this wine is better than the old wine. You can't put this new wine in the skin of the old paradigm. This is the New Wine for the Marriage of the Lamb.

MARY

Mary reveals a core part of being a sharer in the glory. Mary walks in her true identity as an advocate, an intercessor, and a guide for others. As she walks in her true identity a transformation takes place. She takes on the dignity of a royal priesthood. She acts as the "Queen Mother" to the King of Kings. In the process Jesus is transformed from the hidden Messiah of prophecy to the Son of Man, the wonder-working Messiah. And the disciples are transformed into believers.

In order to be a winemaker you have to follow Mary's example. **First you have to face and identify the problem.** You can't fake this. It's essential. You have to know what the right question is in order to know what the right answer is.

Second, you have to listen to the voice of the Lord and do whatever He tells you. Even if that voice says go fill up tubs of water.

Finally, you have to release it all to God and let him do the miraculous part. I have learned that ninety percent of every miracle depends on my sweat, tears, and long obedience. When you give God an offering like that, it becomes wood for a fire. It becomes a sacrifice for the altar and He does the thing that only God can do. God answers with fire. God takes our 90% and makes it 110% or more.

The wedding at Cana continued the "yes" Mary gave to God in Nazareth. Blessed is she who believes. She can say to this mountain, "be cast into the sea." Blessed is she who believes, she can say, "Do whatever he tells you. I know he will do it."

Blessed is she who believes. Because you believed God can turn water into wine.

Intercessor

There is one more piece of this story we need to explore. It is an essential part of the identity of every believer. You are an intercessor. In this story Mary intercedes on behalf of the married couple. Although we don't read the text this way, Mary is actually going to her son as an intermediary and making the case for their need. This is role of the intercessor—a person who "stands in the gap" for someone else.

A big part of our ministry has been strategic prayer. Many, many people come to me and tell me that they are "intercessors" or that they have the "gift" of intercession. Although the Bible gives us a lot of direction about prayer, and the New Testament especially gives us a mandate to pray; there is no place in the New Testament where intercession is set apart as a distinct gift or office. In fact, I have seen a lot of imbalance when a person says they are called to the office of intercession. No one is called to be a mediator as their primary call. Paul reminds us that there is one mediator between God and humanity, Jesus Christ.

But this is where it gets interesting. Because of the Incarnation and the Holy Spirit, Jesus Christ lives in you. Because Jesus is in you, he lives through you.

Jesus the one mediator makes us mediators too.

We are all uniquely called to stand in the gap for others. There have been many moments in my life where God rearranged my schedule and redirected my steps, and then I found later that there was a significant purpose. The most dramatic time this happened was the day before the Boston Bombing terrorist attack. Because of a few surprises one Sunday morning, I found myself needing a change of clothes before I went to a church to speak. There were only a few places open on a Sunday, and so I had to go to the main shopping district on Boylston Street in Boston. That day I did something unusual. I took a picture.

The next morning I discovered that my picture was of the spot where the first bomb exploded, killing three people. I didn't know what was going to happen, but Jesus in me did. Wherever I go Jesus goes with me. We forget that we are accompanied by angels where ever we go. Our very lives can be a prayer. Although the bombing was a tragedy, it might have been much worse.

We cannot be the intermediary between God and humanity, but we can be used to share the work of Jesus in intercession. God wants to share his glory with us, and involve us in the transformation of all creation. This is the beauty of Incarnational reality—Jesus in us redeeming the world. And it is clear in the book of Revelation that this ministry on earth is one of the jobs we will continue in eternity after we finish our work on earth. And as the wedding at Cana shows us, intercession is essentially a creative task.

In the beginning of the ministry of Jesus, the glory of God was revealed when water was turned into wine. Mary played an instrumental part in the miracle. Just like Mary, part of our calling is making wine.

You are more than you think you are.

In our next chapter we will look at the climax of Mary embracing her identity.

TEN

BRIDE

When the soldiers had crucified Jesus they took his garments and made four parts, one for each soldier; also his tunic. But the tunic was without seam, woven from top to bottom; so they said to one another, "Let us not tear it, but cast lots for it to see whose it shall be." This was to fulfill the Scripture,

"They parted my garments among them,
and for my clothing they cast lots."

So the soldiers did this. But standing by the cross of Jesus were his mother, and his mother's sister, Mary the wife of Clopas, and Mary Magdalene. When Jesus saw his mother, and the disciple whom he loved standing near, he said to his mother, "Woman, behold, your son!" Then he said to the disciple, "Behold, your mother!" And from that hour the disciple took her to his own home.

After this Jesus, knowing that all was now finished, said (to fulfill the Scripture), "I thirst." A bowl full of vinegar stood there; so they put a sponge full of the vinegar on hyssop and held it to his mouth. When Jesus had received the vinegar, he said, "It is finished"; and he bowed his head and gave up his spirit.

Since it was the day of Preparation, in order to prevent the bodies from remaining on the cross on the sabbath (for that sabbath was a high day), the Jews asked Pilate that their legs might be broken, and that they might be taken away. So the soldiers came and broke the legs of the first, and of the other who had been crucified with him; but when they came to Jesus and saw that he was already dead, they did not break his legs. But one of the soldiers pierced his side with a spear, and at once there came out blood and water. He who saw it has borne witness—his testimony is true, and he knows that he tells the truth—that you also may believe. For these things took place that the Scripture might be fulfilled, "Not a bone of him shall be broken." And again another Scripture says, "They shall look on him whom they have pierced." —John 19:23-37

A Lamp in the Dark

For many who visit Jerusalem, the Church of the Holy Sepulchre is a big disappointment. Many people imagine an open beautiful space full of prayerful reverence and awe. Instead they find the memorial where Jesus died and rose again in the Muslim market quarter. The church itself is dark, dirty, and overcrowded. It is staffed with pushy priests who manage the crowd. It is famous for competing denominations vying for space. The crowds are full of believers and unbelievers alike. The long barricaded waiting areas make it more like an ancient Disneyland than the place where redemption happened.

Every time I go there, I wonder if no one got the message. **He is not here for he is risen.**

Even so, there are many surprises in the oldest continuous church in Christianity. One surprise is a small oil lamp burning beneath a stone cupola. This little shrine marks the spot where Mary stood on the day of the crucifixion and looked up at her Son on the cross.

In Hebrew the word for truth is "emet." It is made of the first, last, and middle letters of the Hebrew alphabet. In this sense it includes the beginning and the end, the aleph and the tav—or translated into Greek, the alpha and the omega. Symbolically, it presents truth as a tension between two apparent "contradictions." Truth has an element of polarity and tension about it. Jesus is fully divine and fully human—and he is the Truth.

There are some who try to forget that Mary was present at every major event of the New Testament. You notice this especially when you look at depictions of the Day of Pentecost. Protestants emphasize Peter preaching, abstract images of flames, and a male dominated crowd. Catholics on the other hand put Mary right in the center, because Acts points out she was there. Somewhere in the middle is the truth. Truth generally lives in the no-man's-land between two extremes.

But no one can deny that after everyone else left Jesus, at the foot of the cross is his closest friend, John. Along with John are the most devoted of all the female disciples with his aunt, and his Mother. She was here just as she was when she gave birth, when he performed his first miracle, at the mid-point of his ministry, and here at his death. Mary's life is entwined into the fabric of salvation history.

There are many who downplay Christmas and the birth of Jesus because they feel the cross is central to the Christian faith.

John, in his tender personal account, brings a balanced perspective. God became a man, and God became a man through a Woman. By taking on flesh, God made all flesh holy. Jesus was fully man and fully God when he died on the cross. And this fully divine man, condemned unjustly, stripped naked and bleeding, died in the presence of his mother. Imagine the shame and humiliation for both of them.

MARY

Flesh and Spirit

There is a tendency to want to make Jesus more spiritual than he was. Gnosticism is the belief that flesh is evil and spirit is good. It teaches that all reality is a duality between good and evil, light and dark. This kind of belief is called "dualism." Dualism is the core of the gnostic cults that arose around early Christianity, and it is the tendency of modern New Age religious who look to pop psycho-spirituality for their inspiration. It is also a core part of Freemasonry, the modern expression of gnosticism.

When God became a man he undermined the Greek notion that physicality was evil, spirit was good, and that asceticism and denial of the physical reality was the path to enlightenment. At the cross we see a God who not only embraced physicality, He submitted to it. Through the body of Mary God showed us that the physical is spiritual and the spiritual realm dwells in flesh.

Let me say that another way. God touched flesh in the most intimate way possible, and instead of being repulsed and diminished by it God blessed it and made it good. The reality of the Incarnation is Christ in you, the hope of glory. Flesh and spirit cannot be separated.

On the cross the physical body of Jesus permanently altered the spiritual realm.

If you are an artist you need to understand this. The physical work you do has spiritual implications. Your work has been blessed and sanctified because God took on flesh. God became a man to make the creative realm good, and that act was sealed when God embraced the cross.

This was the worst day in Mary's life. She knew it was coming, because at the day of her purification, the old prophet Simeon told her, "A sword will pierce your own heart."³⁴ Although she was warned, I am sure she never expected the grim reality before her.

Five years ago I held a screaming woman in my arms. She was the mother of young man murdered on the streets of Boston. This woman was a close friend and a member of our house of prayer team. I will never forget the sound of her sobs and the look of anguish on her face as we buried her oldest child. Today she is in a long journey of healing. The pain that she experienced is beyond any I have seen a person suffer.

In a similar way, I cannot comprehend the pain Mary felt when the child she carried was falsely accused, publicly mocked, tortured, and then executed before his enemies. Through all of this agony, Mary stood to the end with only a small group of friends.

Behold Your Mother

John's gospel is an amazing piece of literature, and I believe we need to take it at face value. It is the eyewitness account of the disciple whom Jesus loved. He wrote it so the reader would come to believe that Jesus was the Messiah. It is this intimate point of view that makes John's perspective on Mary unique. This intimate moment at the cross between the author, Jesus, and Mary is the center of John's portrait of Mary.

From John we learn that even in the pains of death, Jesus was concerned about the welfare of his mother. Consider that it was the Father of Jesus who commanded, "Honor thy father and mother." At this moment, he honors his mother. He also honors John. In the moment of anguish, Jesus entrusts Mary into the care of John. And from that moment forward, John takes Mary into his home.

---

34   Luke 2:35.

MARY

When God begins something in a person's life, the task is never finished. We are eternal creatures with a never ending history in God. God doesn't use people and then discard them. God begins with a person and then that sanctifying grace continues on forever. God's ways are not the ways of men. God is not focused on completing a project. God is focused on building a new creation that has no end.

The Water and the Blood

And this moment at the cross holds a surprise. In an earlier chapter I pointed out how John parallels the first chapters of his gospel with the poetry at the beginning of Genesis. Throughout this gospel John is attempting to show us that the New Covenant is a New Creation. It is a second chance for humanity. And I mentioned how the theme of water runs through the entire book. The water imagery is used to symbolize two things—the command Jesus holds over the creation, and the movement and presence of the Holy Spirit. In fact, several times we see that Jesus is the giver and releaser of the Holy Spirit through the image of water. For John water and the Holy Spirit are one.

On a cold night in Bethlehem Jesus was born. God opened Mary's womb—to use very Biblical language. And in that moment blood and water flowed. Although later theologians would surmise that Mary remained a virgin throughout her life, the Bible indicates Jesus had a normal birth. The evidence for this is Mary's appearance for ritual cleansing forty days later. She was being purified from the release of blood in the process of childbirth.

Remember what Jesus called his mother at the wedding at Cana? And remember that his ministry was born at that moment with water and wine. Again, Jesus refers to his mother as "Woman." Again Jesus links Mary to Eve. And Jesus presents his mother to his disciple. He is creating a new family on the earth, the family of his Bride. It is the family of those who hear the Word of God and keep it.

And then, Jesus dies. And if you are paying attention to the water in John, this is a critical moment. It parallels a critical moment in Genesis.

God saw that Adam was alone, and it was not good. So God put Adam under a deep sleep. God opened Adam's side and removed a rib. That rib was the raw material for Adam's new wife, Eve. God created a bride for Adam by opening his side.

And after Jesus is dead, a centurion takes a lance and pierces the side of Jesus with his lance. Out of that wound, blood and water flow. In John's first letter he references back to this moment.

> This is he who came by water and blood, Jesus Christ, not with the water only but with the water and the blood. And the Spirit is the witness, because the Spirit is the truth. There are three witnesses, the Spirit, the water, and the blood; and these three agree.[35]

And just as water and blood flowed at his birth, they flowed at his death. And just like Adam, Jesus the New Adam is under the deep sleep of death. God uses a soldier to open up his side. The veil of his temple is penetrated, and blood and water flow. And as John tells us, so does the Holy Spirit. God is creating a bride for his Son. John brings us back to the overarching narrative of the Bible here at the cross.

And who is standing there when the blood and water flow?

Mary.

---

35 1 John 5:6-8.

MARY

In this stark and emotional moment, John the poet and story teller links Mary to Eve and to the Church. She is the first to be sprinkled by the water and the blood. She is the first to be incorporated into the Bride of Christ, even as she has already been the "spouse of the Holy Spirit." This moment is a bookend in the Gospel of John with the wedding at Cana. It helps us see why God would put his Son and the Woman center stage at the wedding at Cana, and why that first miracle had to be water into wine. The wine of His cup will never run out and his Bride will forever enjoy the best wine that has been saved to the end.

An angel invited Mary to a destiny that was full of grace. She experienced moments throughout her life where the grace flowed, like at the wedding. And then she had other moments. Moments when she was frightened that her son was missing and found him teaching priests in the temple. And she was frustrated when the demands of being Messiah made it too hard to be a part of her family.

At the cross Mary received a new family—a family born by water and the Holy Spirit. Mary received a new son, John. And Mary was no longer the bride of Joseph, she was the Bride of Christ. Her new family would gather around her in an upper room, and they would all share the outpouring that she had already experienced. They would all be connected to her, because in a very real way, she was the mother of the Body of the Lord.

Sometimes when God calls us, we are shocked by how the call plays out in our lives. God is always calling us to more than we think or imagine. God is always seeing more than we believe is possible. His plan for us is to become more than we think we can become.

Mary, the little girl from Nazareth became the Mother of the Messiah and the Bride of Christ. It messes with your reality as much as Mary is God's mom. It says a lot about Jesus and the multidimensional reality he lived in—relational, eternal, human, and divine.

So what does that say about us?

You are being called to fullness.
You are being called to greatness.

You are being called to the perplexing multidimensional reality where you can be the church, you can be a Bride, you can be a son, you can be royalty, and you can be a servant. God wants to invite you into the fellowship He created when He entered space and time.

Greatness happens when you say, "Let it be to me according to your word." As Bonhoeffer said, this is the moment when Jesus says, "Come and die." Mary's first death happened when she surrendered her plan and her womb to the Holy Spirit. But she didn't receive it all at that moment. The ongoing sanctifying grace of God worked in and through her until she also became a participant in her son's death. That's when all her hopes and dreams died. You cannot do anything great for God until you come to this place. That's the place where you say, "It is finished." It's in that moment that the blood and water begins to flow. That's when God can make new wine out of the tears in the sorrows of your life. That's when death and resurrection begin to operate.

The cross is the beginning of discovering who you really are. This is the moment when you truly can listen to God and do what He tells you. This is the moment when that outrageous and fierce call of God on your life receives the spark of resurrection power. It is in dying that we live, and in living that we are born to eternal life.

MARY

This is the grace that flows and makes a place where you belong in God's family. This is when you become the Bride that the Father is seeking for his Son. That's the moment you can begin to do the impossible because the grace of God has gone before you. And you can say like Mary, you have been full of grace, and that grace will bring you to the place of triumph.

ELEVEN

CROWNED

Then God's temple in heaven was opened, and the ark of his covenant was seen within his temple; and there were flashes of lightning, loud noises, peals of thunder, an earthquake, and heavy hail.

And a great portent appeared in heaven, a woman clothed with the sun, with the moon under her feet, and on her head a crown of twelve stars; she was with child and she cried out in her pangs of birth, in anguish for delivery.

And another portent appeared in heaven; behold, a great red dragon, with seven heads and ten horns, and seven diadems upon his heads. His tail swept down a third of the stars of heaven, and cast them to the earth. And the dragon stood before the woman who was about to bear a child, that he might devour her child when she brought it forth; she brought forth a male child, one who is to rule all the nations with a rod of iron, but her child was caught up to God and to his throne, and the woman fled into the wilderness, where she has a place prepared by God, in which to be nourished for one thousand two hundred and sixty days.

Now war arose in heaven, Michael and his angels fighting against the dragon; and the dragon and his angels fought, but they were defeated and there was no longer any place for them in heaven. And the great dragon was thrown down, that ancient serpent, who is called the Devil and Satan, the deceiver of the whole world—he was thrown down to the earth, and his angels were thrown down with him. And I heard a loud voice in heaven, saying, "Now the salvation and the power and the kingdom of our God and the authority of his Christ have come, for the accuser of our brethren has been thrown down, who accuses them day and night before our God. —Revelation 11:19-12:10

Earlier I mentioned that all the threads in the beginning of Genesis eventually re-emerge in Revelation. Mary's story ends here, in the place of triumph.

Symbol, Themes, and Language

The book of Revelation is packed with symbols. All of the previous chapters in this book have unpacked different symbols the Bible uses in regard to Mary: Ark, Mother, Woman, Eve, Bride, and now Crowned.

God speaks in symbols. So often over the past 20 years of teaching I have heard the phrase "Oh, that is just a symbol." Many believers think that symbolic language and ideas are dispensable, and can be interpreted any way. And because of this, there is a great ignorance of symbolic language. But we forget that words themselves are symbols, and God revealed himself as the Word. So God enfleshed himself in symbol. Symbols carry the Glory.

On a recent speaking tour I stood in a stunning chapel with some of the finest stained glass in the world. The chapel was owned by an international missions organization. Here, as I have seen so many times before, an evangelical organization has defaced or covered up an amazing work of Christian art. In this case, the owners hung a blank screen in front of a large window to cover up images of St. Christopher carrying Jesus and the Virgin Mary surrounded by angels that represented all the arts and sciences.

After some coaxing, I asked my hosts to raise the screen so I could see the window.

"Why do you want to do *that*?" my hosts asked me.

"It's an amazing work of art, and I want to see it." I replied.

With shock my friends replied, "That window is evil. It represents Masonic symbolism and pagan gods and goddesses, it's a portal for the demonic."

I have heard these outcries again and again with ministries afraid of demonic strongholds being established through image and symbol.

After a very heated conversation, I explained you cannot have a ministry in the arts and to artists if you believe all symbolic language is evil. You cannot tell people to paint if paintings become tools of the devil. So many in our day have lost the ability to recognize the story of the Bible and our salvation in the language of symbol. This language has Jewish roots, it was born in the Tabernacle, and continued and expanded into the Church.

As our conversation continued, I asked my friends if I could pray. They agreed but they were uneasy. The chapel had been in a large home for orphan children, and as I prayed I began to sense there was something wrong. God began to give me "words of knowledge." There had been a history of various types of abuse, both physical and sexual here. We began to pray and I took the time to address the real sin that happened here.

There *was* a demonic stronghold in the building, but it was not there because of images and symbols. It was sin that had brought a curse on the land. Satan would love it if we continued to smash windows and churches and never dealt with the root causes. He gets a double victory—destroying signposts that bear the testimony of Jesus, and causing infighting among believers over trivial matters.

After my prayer, my friends immediately noticed the peace that entered the room. Our ministry team has prayed all over the world and often dealt with secret sin. In each case we see changes. This prayer works because we apply the power of the cross and resurrection to physical places and spaces. This is possible because God entered this physical world and lived here. This is the power of the Incarnation, and the power of understanding symbol.[36]

Thankfully our time in the chapel with my friends ended on a happy note. They later invited me back to talk about symbolic language and the arts to the entire mission.

Apocalyptic Masterpiece

It bears repeating: the Bible is the premier masterwork of literature in human history. It is ultimately a work of art. The Book of Revelation ends the Bible by taking that art form into a different direction. All of the threads, ideas, and themes of the Bible get revisited in Revelation's chapters and forms that final border on this glorious tapestry. At face value, the Book of Revelation is a series of visions given to us by a seer named John. And because they are visions, they are full of symbolic language. Most of the symbolic language is easy to sort out, but here and there the references are mysterious. I have spent three decades meditating on the Book of Revelation. I am convinced that the writer is sometimes describing things that he himself didn't understand.

---

36   Leanne Payne wrote extensively about the healing power of symbol in her books *Restoring the Christian Soul through Healing Prayer and Healing Presence*.

And there is another dimension to this book. It represents a genre of literature that flourished in Israel from about the time of Daniel until around the second century. It is called "Apocalyptic" literature. That's why the Latin title for this book is the *Apocalypse*. Parts of this book use established code language that we see in other books that exist outside the Bible. Some of the better known examples of apocalyptic books are the Book of Enoch and some of the excerpts from the Dead Sea Scrolls. The symbols in Revelation do make reference to contemporary events—like the Roman Empire and the persecution of the early church. The code language was often used to protect both the writer and the hearer from persecution, while sharing a dangerous message.

Often Apocalyptic literature refers back to the past, comments on the present, and does this using language prophesying the future. Because of this multidimensional quality, Revelation can be a source of endless study. And if you have a distorted understanding of image and symbol, Revelation will lead that study into all kinds of crazy conclusions. In the United States this distortion has produced a cottage industry of all kinds of end-time books, TV programs, movies, and new theories about the return of Jesus.

A Break in the Wrong Place

Like all of the Bible, the chapter and verse headings were added centuries after the writing of the original text. Verse markings appeared after the invention of the printing press as reference marks for typesetting. The chapters were added to help the copyists in monasteries find their place when doing their work.

Over time Revelation was divided up various ways. Our current chapter headings were added in the 13th century by Stephen

MARY

Langton.[37] Many of the divisions (and now additional subheadings inserted by publishers and editors) are in the wrong place and sometimes break up important thoughts. Many places in the Book of Revelation are hard to understand, and an incorrect break in a thought will add to the confusion. Revelation chapter 12 is a great example. I believe the chapter should begin one verse earlier in 11:19.

How do I know? One of the great resources we have are lectionaries. Lectionaries are books used for the public reading of Scripture, and many of them are very old. When the church read this section of the Bible in public, it chose to begin the passage with Revelation 11:19. If you read this passage out loud, that break makes a lot of sense, and helps us really understand what is happening here.

God's temple in heaven is opened and we see the Ark of the Covenant. This is the last time the Ark appears in the Bible. The Ark is accompanied by signs of God's glory we mentioned earlier: thunder, earthquakes, fire, hail, lightning, and voices. This echoes not just the temple of Solomon, but also the experience Moses had on the mountain when he received the blueprint for the Tabernacle and the Ark. Again, God is revealing his glory. Once again we are about to get a revelation. Whenever we encounter the Glory we are going to learn something about God's identity. God has brought a person into the glory.

An important sign appears, and the sign is a woman. And this woman is clothed with glory. There is only one other person in the New Testament described in a similar way—Jesus in the first chapter of Revelation and Jesus on the mountain of Transfiguration. She looks like Jesus. The Woman is clothed with the Sun. She stands on

---

37 B. Metzger, *The early versions of the New Testament: Their origin, transmission and limitations*, Oxford University Press (1977), p.347.

the moon—representing a place above the created order. And on her head she is wearing a crown made of twelve stars.

The images in her description echo Joseph's dream of the Moon and the Sun and 12 stars bowing down to him. The people in that dream were Jacob, Rachel and Joseph's brothers.[38] They represent the entire nation of Israel. This woman is clothed with all the glory of Israel. But she is also pregnant. She is about to give birth. She is a glorious mother. And waiting in the lurch is a great red dragon, licking his lips, waiting to eat the baby as soon as he is delivered.

Wow, what an image!

> I will put enmity between you and the woman,
> between your offspring and hers;
> he will strike your head and you will strike his heel.[39]

Once again we see an echo of the beginning of Genesis where the promised child of the woman will crush the head of the serpent. We see a direct reference to Isaiah 14 where Lucifer is cast from heaven with a third of the angels. And we see echoes of all the Messianic prophecies. The child to be born will rule the nations with mighty power.

Who is the Woman?

In Protestant seminary we were taught that the woman was Israel, the Church, and possibly the early Christian community in Rome. And absolutely, this woman was not Mary!

If you take the chapter at face value, it is easy to recognize Mary in

---

38   Genesis 37:9.

39   Genesis 3:15.

the Woman. She is the Ark, the daughter of Israel, the Mother of the Messiah, the New Eve, and the Bride, the Church. Now she is the Woman clothed with the Son. We are now getting an image of her, remaining on earth after Jesus is taken up into heaven. She is now mothering His children. And they are her children. In this scene we are seeing all the themes begin to come together.

Sometimes the book of Revelation gives us a vision of earthly things from a spiritual point of view. It's almost like a backstage pass where we see what's really going on behind human events. Here we are getting a glimpse of Mary from the cosmic point of view. She has received divine favor—a crown in heaven. This favor, this grace, God is using to destroy that ancient serpent the Devil. And all the political powers of the satanic realm are conspiring to kill the woman's child. Herod's attempt to murder the baby was foiled by an escape into the Egyptian desert.

The Government of God

Although the stars in Mary's crown can represent the twelve tribes of Israel, in Revelation the number twelve is a symbol for government. We are seeing two kingdoms collide, the government of man and the Government of God. The woman is the representation of the Kingdom of God over all creation. The dragon's seven diadems in contrast represent human government, and most directly, the seven hills of Rome. At the time of the book's writing the dragon was an image of the Pax Romana keeping peace through brute force and fear.

Recently I heard a leader in my city say that the culture war was over, and that we need to embrace the advancing non-Biblical sexual agenda. He was wrong; here in Revelation we see the culture war continues to the end of time.

Earlier I wrote that the Ark is the portable throne of God. The vision begins with God revealing his throne with a release of glory. And what is this throne? It is an ark made of flesh. This government is established on a girl who said "yes" to God. God's throne and God's authority are established when we listen to God and do what he tells us. The rule and reign of God are established on this true blessedness. And any time we go low and say yes to God we are coming into opposition against the governments of man that are built on pride, power, arrogance, and physical strength.

The Woman clothed with the Sun went low, emptied herself, and was filled with God. As a result, God used her to establish the New Covenant, begin to undo the bad mothering of Eve, crush the serpent's head, and bring forth the Ruler of the Nations.

God writes straight with a crooked line. He made peace by establishing a creative solution to humanity's greatest problem. Rather than using force to impose his will, He took the risk and shared his glory. God did something completely different in this New Covenant. The New Covenant is about people giving birth to other holy people. It's not about programs or things. God first made a holy person, and in the process He gave birth to a Son who made a holy people.

God won a very big victory by choosing to use a very little weapon: the girl who said "yes." He chooses the foolish things, the worthless things, the things no one else would choose. He shamed the wise, the philosophers, and the strong when He decided to enter the world as a baby. I guess it's no surprise that no other human being has inspired more works of art, more hymns and poetry, more wayside shrines and mumbled prayers than this little girl from Nazareth.

MARY

Bigger Than You Think You Are

Maybe we have missed something in our quest for doctrinal purity. Earlier in this book I said you cannot say anything about Mary that doesn't also say something about Jesus, and something about you and me.

I don't know if Mary ever read the Book of Revelation. In all likelihood, her life ended before it was written. As I have worked on this book, I have pondered the things John said about Mary. These things were written by a man who lived with her and knew her on a day to day basis. He knew that if Jesus was who he said he was, then this woman was more than she thought she was. Whenever you do something great for God, you yourself know that you only did what was your duty at the moment. There is nothing heroic in obeying the call of God. But from God's perspective we are doing things that have cosmic implications. We are all altering the fabric of the universe. And sadly, we do it even though we do not know who we really are. We are crowned with glory and honor, seated in heavenly places, and He has put all things under our feet.[40]

Every creative person is called to discover and agree with their God given identity. Your identity as a priest to a visual multi-sensory culture is dependent on your identity in Christ. Your inner life determines your creative output. The world depends on you knowing who you really are.

Let me say that again.

The world depends on you knowing who you really are.

The Serpent works very hard to keep creative people in an endless

---

40 Colossians 3:1, 1 Peter 2:9, Hebrews 2:8.

identity struggle. If you are not sure who you are, you will never be able to move forward. If you are confused, you can never bring clarity to others. Our God is not the author of confusion.[41]

We have now spent a lot of time exploring different facets of Mary's identity in God. She is full of grace, the New Eve, the Bride, the Blessed among Women, and the one Clothed with the Sun, Crowned with twelve stars. Every one of these titles can be applied to you.

Every thing the Bible says about Mary says something about who you are.
- You were created to be full of the Holy Spirit.
- You are the recipient of grace.
- You are the New Creation.
- You are the Bride of Christ.
- You are blessed and highly favored.
- You are blessed when you hear the word of God and keep it.
- You are a member of the family of Jesus.
- You are called to make the Word flesh.

Martin Luther once mistakenly said "the church is my mother, and she is a whore." Revelation gives us a very different picture. **The church is our Mother, and she is a Virgin.** God's perspective is so different from ours. This New Covenant is about who you are and where you belong. This New Covenant is about a new family and identity. It really is about belonging. You belong to Jesus, and like John, you behold your mother. The goal is to follow her example.

Mary went low with her Son. In rising he brought creation up, and he brought his mother with him.

---

41   I Corinthians 14:33.

MARY

TWELVE

OFFSPRING

And I heard a loud voice in heaven, saying, "Now the salvation and the power and the kingdom of our God and the authority of his Christ have come, for the accuser of our brethren has been thrown down, who accuses them day and night before our God.

And they have conquered him by the blood of the Lamb and by the word of their testimony, for they loved not their lives even unto death. Rejoice then, O heaven and you that dwell therein! But woe to you, O earth and sea, for the devil has come down to you in great wrath, because he knows that his time is short!"

And when the dragon saw that he had been thrown down to the earth, he pursued the woman who had borne the male child. But the woman was given the two wings of the great eagle that she might fly from the serpent into the wilderness, to the place where she is to be nourished for a time, and times, and half a time. The serpent poured water like a river out of his mouth after the woman, to sweep her away with the flood. But the earth came to the help of the woman, and the earth opened its mouth and swallowed the river which the dragon had poured from his mouth. Then the dragon was angry with the woman, and went off to make war on the rest of her offspring, on those who keep the commandments of God and bear testimony to Jesus. And he stood on the sand of the sea.
—Revelation 12:10-17

MARY

When God began speaking to me and our team about Mary, I struggled. My first thought was "Now *what* will people think?"

Sometimes doing God's will comes before understanding God's will. I spent several years pondering and meditating on all of the Scriptures that have made the foundation of this book. After all this prayer and meditation I had a revelation. **Jesus loves his mother.**

We get so caught up in doctrines and theology that we forget that something very real and organic happened when God became a man. Jesus created a new family based on spiritual DNA.

We are all connected. As we saw in the story of Bezalel, God doesn't deposit into someone for that person alone. Bezalel was given the gift of teaching so he could impart the gifts he received into another generation. In this New Covenant, Mary's gift was to give birth. Rather than students she received offspring. Every time a new believer rises from the waters of baptism they are born to eternal life, and born into an eternal family. And they receive the water of the Holy Spirit and the blood of Christ in Holy Communion. When you are welcomed into a family, you are welcomed to a family dinner table.

An Identity of Belonging

This sense of belonging is the heart of the gospel. Your identity is shaped by belonging to God's family. One of the saddest unintended consequences of the Reformation has been divorce and division. There is a sense that you are disconnected from others unless they subscribe to a certain set of doctrinal standards. We have lost the sense that we are organically connected to those who went before us, to Mary, to Peter, to John, and to all those who were part of that original family. God is looking for a Bride for His Son, a family.

There is a war against life, against birth, and against women and children. I know because I worked for many years in the Pro-Life movement. Why does the devil hate new life? Every new life is a potential glory bearer. Every new life can be fruitful and multiply. Every new life is a little creator. Every new life is another bearer of the Image of God and could potentially become like Mary—full of grace, crowned with glory, and crushing serpents.

And every time someone bears the glory of God, a bit more of the identity of God is revealed. Remember, Glory is about identity. When God shares his glory with you, he is sharing a part of this identity with you. The goal is for you to be a reflection of God.

At the beginning of this book I quoted the prayer Jesus prayed in John 17.

> The glory that you have given me **I have given them**, so that they may be one, as we are one, I in them and you in me, that they may become completely one, so that the world may know that you have sent me and have loved them even as you have loved me. Father, I desire that those also, whom you have given me, may be with me where I am, to see my glory, which you have given me because you loved me before the foundation of the world.[42]

Our book ends with a commission. Will you be a glory bearer?

If you say "yes," Revelation 12 gives you three directions on how to succeed.

You will overcome by the Blood of the Lamb.
You will overcome by the word of your testimony.
You will overcome by not loving your life more than death.

---

42 John 17:21-24 NRSVA. Emphasis mine.

MARY

The Blood of the Lamb
First, you have to come under the blood of the Lamb. This is a reference to Passover where the blood of a lamb was placed on the door of the house. The angel of death saw the blood and did not touch that house. In the same way, when we confess with our mouth Jesus is Lord, and believe in our hearts God raised him from the dead, His blood also covers us.

You have to be in a relationship with God first.

Then you can overcome.

But overcoming is also about walking out that process of grace. And that means returning to God, and reapplying that blood again and again as a means of grace. And once again, that blood is accompanied by water. The Bible says you need to be baptized. He came by water and the blood. We overcome by water and the blood.

The word of your testimony.
The second part of overcoming is telling your story. There is power in the word of testimony. And telling your story means painting your picture, writing your song, developing your screenplay, designing your game, or dancing your dance. The testimony of Jesus is the spirit of prophecy, and when you tell your story you have a cosmic influence, rewriting the rhythm of the spiritual realm all around you.

> This is an extraordinary moment, not unlike the day Gutenberg published his Bible. He did this the same year Columbus sailed to the New World, and within 25 years a dramatic shaking had occurred in Europe. Somewhere in the past 25 years we experienced a similar moment when civilizations, technology and culture all collided. We are living

in the moment of interconnected, decentralized information. All of this powerful information is being transmitted through images and stories, not through words. Many do not grasp the dramatic shift that is happening all around us. Knowledge, and access to knowledge, is increasing every second.

Actually, there are many who do understand, and they are making use of this new power. There are leaders who are using the Internet, Computer Generated Image technology, video gaming, cinema, social networking, and personal technology to shape reality, ideas, and perceptions. In skilled hands trends, fashions, markets, and elections can all be manipulated seamlessly. Media is the water in the fishbowl. It determines the temperature, current, and food that impact us, the fish.

It is the moment of the story, and the storyteller. The one who overcomes in this moment is the one most gifted in telling a story. This is the moment of the artist. It is the moment of the troubadour, the dramatist, and the designer. It is the moment of the film maker, the novelist, the dancer, the puppeteer, the poet, and the painter. The storytellers have been set apart for this moment. If this is you, then this is your day.[43]

God needs men and women who are fully committed to bearing the testimony of Jesus through the work of their hands. This is the most exciting time in history to release creative output.

Not loving your life.

Judy Garland once said, "Why be a second rate version of somebody else when you can be a first rate version of yourself." She was talking about her imitators. Part of dying to yourself is taking the risk of putting all that God put in you out before other people. When I

---

43 Otto, Christ, *An Army Arising*, 14.

meet and talk with artists, you would be surprised at how many are afraid to really put their creation out before people. It is much safer to make a hack version of something with a Christian veneer. Risk is about dying to yourself and putting it out before others.

I have been privileged to meet many amazing creative professionals in my work. And of all the stories I have heard, the story of Project Dance encapsulates these three principles. Cheryl Cutlip, the founder of Project Dance shared her story with me:

> The very first Project Dance New York was certainly unique. At the time I didn't realize the significance of this movement being birthed in the city. Now, 13 years later, I'm able to see more clearly why that battle was so intense.
>
> Following the events of 911, my husband and I wanted to see hope and healing for New Yorkers. Dance is my passion and felt strongly that dance could be used to bring a bit of joy amidst a very broken people. I called on friends like Randy to travel to New York and share the message of hope through dance.
>
> Throughout the process of planning this event, I was able to convince about 50 friends to join together and dance in Times Square as a sign of God's love for New York City.
>
> The permit process was new to us and we had filed an application with our local community board. They had approved the event and we were so happy to continue our planning. 2 weeks prior to the event we had yet to receive our permit. I called the community board and asked if we could be issued the approval paperwork. That's when I learned that we needed the approval of the city in order to proceed. The board approval only meant that our application would be

viewed by the city. That didn't mean that we had the final "yes" for our event.

Of course, you can imagine how quickly our hearts sank as we realized that dancers were already booked to travel to New York and yet we, without realizing it, hadn't been fully approved.

These next 2 weeks would prove to be challenging! Ron and I began calling the city to try to understand where our application was in the process of approval. No one returned our calls. After a few days of desperately trying to reach the city we realized that we were going to have to physically go to the city and find a representative.

The first day we arrived there was no one who could help us or direct us to any help. The second day we arrived we were told that we wouldn't be seen about our permit. The third day we arrived we were told to come back in a few days. As you can imagine, we are feeling less and less confident.

Finally, we were able to meet with the city representative of "events". She proceeded to tell us that she was not going to able to approve our event due to the location we'd requested. The particular location was under a "hold" due to a law suit between the city and another organization. Because of the law suit they were not allowed to issue any street activities until this case was resolved. She said that we could appeal but we would probably not be successful.

Now, just days before our first event, we were getting even more stressed out.

We did appeal and it was denied.

MARY

Finally, we went back to the city to beg for a different location for our same event. As I sat down in the office of the mayor with the city representative I began telling her more of our story; why we wanted to dance in the city and what we were hoping to achieve with our project. I shared with her that I was a performer with The Rockettes and that some Rockettes along with some performers from the Broadway community as well as some friends from other states wanted to give back after the events of 911. We wanted to dance for the people of New York and share hope and healing.

What happened next surprised me. She said, "I know you". I felt embarrassed that I didn't recognize her, especially since she was part of the mayor's office. She had been invited to a recent high profile performance in town where The Rockettes had performed. At the after party she reminded me that I had spoken to her and allowed her to cut in front of me in the line for food. I had not remembered our meeting but was so thankful that she had remembered me. After sharing a bit more with her, she approved our event to take place on 44th and Broadway from 8:00am to 8:00pm. We were given the approval to hold our 12 hour concert to bring hope and healing to New Yorkers.

I left there on top of the world. However, little did I know that we weren't there yet.

Now just a few days from the event we still needed our sound permit. This permit was to be obtained through the NYPD. Upon the city's approval we would now be able to successfully gain our sound permit which would allow for amplification of sound. I began calling the NYPD to set up a time to get the permit. Again, no returned phone calls. So, again, Ron and I physically began visiting the NYPD. The first time we arrived, the detective was not there. We tried to get an idea of when he would be there so that we could return for the permitting process.

Finally, we caught him in his office. We knocked on his closed door and a deep, loud voice came through from inside...."Go away!". Completely afraid we answered back, we need to speak with you. He cracked open the door and said "what do you want?" We said that we had gotten the city approval for our street activity and needed to get our sound permit.

He asked us to sit down in his office where we could see our permit on top of his desk. Then he said, we are not going to approve this event. We mentioned that the city had approved the event and therefore we felt it was in our scope to also now obtain the sound permit. He said, no, I will not shut down Times Square on a Saturday for 12 hours. This too much to ask for this city and no one shuts down Times Square. He sat back in his chair and lowered his glasses and asked, "Who do you know? Are you the mayor's daughter? Who do you know?" I said, no sir, I know God! He said, "Don't give me that praying stuff, who do you know?" I went on to tell him that I didn't have any connections with the city or their officials but that we wanted to dance for the people of New York and try to restore hope to the city.

Reluctantly, he called down to the city to double check that there hadn't been a mistake. The city responded with, yes, we have approved this event. The detective had no choice at the point but to go ahead with the sound permit.

What we didn't know at the time was what that also meant for our event. The NYPD, upon approval, would now provide security for our event throughout the day, offer us barricades

MARY

to block off traffic from the street during our event, provide the no parking signs for the street as well as the sound permit.

So, just 1 day before our event, all permits were in order and we were able to host the very first Project Dance event.

This event has now taken place each April for the past 13 years. We often revisit this story as a sign of God's love for New York and the ability of dance to open hearts to a message of hope and healing. The Mayor's office has also given Project Dance New York a proclamation, PROJECT DANCE DAY! We are humbly blessed to host this event annually in the heart of New York.

As we've ventured cities around the world, we've had similar experiences with local city governments. Each time, God has shown favor and we've been able to host events in prominent downtown locations all over the world. When our event was scheduled to take place in the Toronto there was a city wide government strike that should have effected our event. Project Dance was the only event able to take place during the strike. When the Pope visited Sydney Australia during the same weekend as Project Dance we received a call from the City of Sydney informing us that the Pope had overridden all permits in order to reserve all prominent locations. Our event was cancelled by the City. Miraculously, Project Dance still took place.

Events have taken place in New York, Sydney, Los Angeles, Hong Kong, Toronto, Brisbane, Jerusalem, Atlanta, Houston, Manila, Greenville, Kansas City, London, Puerto Rico, Costa Rica, Orlando, Penang, Washington DC, and Phoenix.

I hope you are encouraged by our story. It's a complete honor to serve The Lord and his heart through the unspoken and universal language of dance. I've learned that people all over the world share in the love and appreciation for dance. I've learned that hearts are opened by the beauty of dance and able to see and hear God's love through it. I've learned that there is a unique essence of God's presence "on the streets."

Cheryl took a big risk, bore the testimony of Jesus, and has been telling that story all over the world. Amazing things happen when mighty women say "yes" to God.

John, in his first letter, told us he was passing on a legacy:

> That which was from the beginning, which we have heard, which we have seen with our eyes, which we have looked upon and touched with our hands, concerning the word of life—the life was made manifest, and we saw it, and testify to it, and proclaim to you the eternal life which was with the Father and was made manifest to us—that which we have seen and heard we proclaim also to you, so that you may have fellowship with us; and our fellowship is with the Father and with his Son Jesus Christ.[44]

Mary's DNA is in you. Just as God shared his glory with her and started a revolution, so God has shared his glory with you.

This is your inheritance, to pass on what you have received. To be fruitful and multiply and transform the world through your creative output. The word of life has been made manifest and this life is alive in you. God is calling you to do greater things than Jesus did, by hearing the word and doing it. This is your destiny, to share the glory that God has shared with you until it covers the earth as the waters cover the sea.

---

44   I John 1:1-3.

MARY

Abba, I pray for every person who reads this book. Go deep into their heart and speak to them about who they are. Reveal to them your glory, and in doing so, may they make the Word flesh. May they be glory bearers. May they be living thrones in the earth to make a way for the coming of the Lord.

Let it be to us according to your Word. Amen.

POSTLUDE

It's about people.

The New Covenant is about people. It's about being connected.

The story of Mary is about God shifting the center of his mercy from an inanimate object that was carried by priests to the bodies of human beings—who become both priest and temple. By the Holy Spirit, God now dwells in the hearts of men and women.

Mary is a reminder that out of fear for God, we have to honor those whom He chooses. In the New Covenant we are organically connected to all who have gone before us.

I'm not proposing that we return to the late medieval religion where we pray to saints rather than with them. Before the Reformation things were out of order. But in their zeal the reformers replaced one disorder with another. And that disorder is playing out in all our lives today. We can keep peace with this, or we can make peace and seek God's order. Shalom is the presence of order. And disconnection and brokenness are not Shalom. I sometimes wonder what some of my friends are going to do on the day of judgment when Jesus asks them why they said what they said about his mom. When I was a kid the best way to get a black eye was to pick on someone's mom.

MARY

In an age where many families are strained or broken, and where many feel as though they have no place to belong, God has given you a family. And that family is good.

God is building his throne in the earth. He is building an Ark of His Presence. That Ark is built in human bodies. It is built in a holy people.

From a covenant focused on law and holy objects we move to a covenant of Word and Holy People. You are good, because Jesus called you out, set you apart, crowned you with glory, and made you a priest to serve others. When this truth gets settled in you your creative output is going to change, your reality is going to shift, and you are going to start shifting the realities of others.

Yes, but how?

In the next book in this series we are going to look at how God becomes flesh in dramatic language and imparts grace to us. God has devised a way to transcend time, space, language, and culture to continually remind us who we are and where we belong. We have looked at how God shares his glory, now we are going to look at how God shares his grace.

ACKNOWLEDGMENTS

Every book involves many hands. I am learning every time how this cannot be a solitary process.

Once again, thank you Nancy Mari for your editorial help. Thank you Jordan Easley for helping review the manuscript.

Special thanks to Jerry and Elizabeth Averill who allowed me to use their home in Linlithgow, Scotland to do most of the writing. The three months away helped speed up the process. Thank you to my friends at the National Library of Scotland who helped with some research.

Thank you Jennie Fournier and our prayer team who interceded for me while I wrote this book.

Thank you to Ed and Ethel Doolittle who made a space for me to do the final rewrites in their home.

Special thanks to the Belonging House board for your support in many ways this time around.

And of course, thank you Blessed Lady.

WORKS CITED

Ambrose, and Ide M. Ni Riain. *Commentary of Saint Ambrose on the Gospel according to Saint Luke*. Dublin: Halcyon, 2001

Brown, Rachel Fulton, "Mary in the Scriptures: The Unexpurgated Tradition" part of the Theotokos Lectures in Theology 2014, Marquette University, Milwaukee, Wisconsin.

Hahn, Scott; Mitch, Curtis (2010-06-14). The Ignatius Catholic Study Bible New Testament (Kindle Locations 8229-8239). Ignatius Press. Kindle Edition.

Justin Martyr, *Dialogue with Trypho*, Chapter C. Christian Classics Ethereal Library, CCEL.org.

Kittel, Gerhard, G. W. Bromiley, and Gerhard Friedrich. Theological Dictionary of the New Testament. Grand Rapids, Mich: Eerdmans, 1964.

Lewis, C. S. (2009-06-03). Weight of Glory (Collected Letters of C.S. Lewis), HarperCollins. Kindle Edition.

Metzger, Bruce, *The early versions of the New Testament: Their origin, transmission and limitations*, Oxford University Press (1977).

Otto, Christ John, *An Army Arising: Why Artists are on the Frontline of the Next Move of God*, Boston: Belonging House Creative, 2013.

Society of St. Francis, David Stancliffe, and Tristam. Celebrating Common Prayer. London: Mowbray, 1994.

If you enjoyed this book, you may enjoy other books
by Christ John Otto:

***An Army Arising: Why Artists Are on the Frontline
of the Next Move of God.***

Bezalel: Redeeming a Renegade Creation

Be Not Afraid: An Advent Devotional

All available on amazon.com

CPSIA information can be obtained
at www.ICGtesting.com
Printed in the USA
LVOW04s1945220117
521785LV00014BB/1010/P